Mortars

MORTARS

Ian V. Hogg

The Crowood Press

First published in 2001 by
The Crowood Press Ltd
Ramsbury, Marlborough
Wiltshire SN8 2HR

British Library Cataloguing-in-Publication Data
A catalogue record for this book is available from the British Library.

ISBN 1 86126 419 4

Typeset by Textype Typesetters, Cambridge

Printed and bound in Great Britain by Antony Rowe Ltd, Chippenham, Wiltshire

Contents

Dedication

For Herbert L. Feldman, a long-standing and long-suffering acquaintance whom I have shamefully neglected, in the hope that this humble offering might go some way to recompense you for your patience.

'No-one has endurance like the man who sells insurance.'

1 The Siege Mortar

The mortar is a strictly defined piece of ordnance; the term means a weapon which fires projectiles at angles of elevation greater than 45 degrees, and which thus has a high trajectory that takes the projectile over intervening crests or cover to drop steeply down onto an otherwise inaccessible target. Nevertheless, and in spite of this, the general expression 'mortar' calls to mind the infantry smoothbore weapon, loaded at the muzzle and capable of being dismantled and carried about by its squad. By and large, this description suffices for most of them, but as we shall see, some mortars are more heavy and complicated than is commonly supposed.

MOHAMMED THE MORTAR MAN

Exactly who was the first man to come up with the idea of elevating a cannon so as to drop the projectile down onto somebody else's head is difficult to say, but there seems to be a good case for crediting it to the Emperor Mohammed II, Sultan of Turkey, during his fifty-three-day Siege of Constantinople in 1453. A manuscript by a Greek scribe, dated 1467, relates how the Emperor, confronted by a Greek fleet which arrived and anchored off the Golden Horn,

> ... turned his attention to the invention of another machine. He called together those who made his guns and demanded of them if it were not possible to fire upon the ships anchored at the entrance to the port, so as to sink them to the bottom. They made answer that there were no cannon capable of producing such an effect, adding that the walls of Galata hindered them on all sides. The Emperor then proposed to them a different mode of proceeding and a totally new description of a gun, of which the form should be

A sixteenth-century engraving of a siege, showing the guns battering the walls by direct fire, the mortars throwing bombs over the wall and into the fortress, and, in the foreground, a trench being excavated to the fortress wall for the final assault.

7

a little modified so as to enable it to throw its shot to a great height that, in falling, it might strike the vessel in the middle and sink her. He explained to them in what manner, by certain proportions calculated and based upon analogy, such a machine would act against the shipping, and these on reflection saw the possibility of the thing, and they made a species of cannon after the outline which the Emperor had made for them. Having next considered the ground, they placed it a little below the Galata Point on a ridge which rose a little opposite the ships. Having placed it well and pointed it in the air according to the proper calculations, they applied the match and the mortar threw its stone to a great height, then falling, it missed the ships the first time and pitched very near them into the sea. They then changed the direction of the mortar a little and threw a second stone. This, after rising to an immense height, fell with great noise and violence and struck a vessel amidships, shattering it, sunk it to the bottom, killed some of the sailors and drowned the rest, only a few saved themselves by swimming to the other ships and nearer galleys.

After this, the idea seems to have taken some time to spread to Europe, but by the end of the sixteenth century the mortar had become a fairly commonplace siege weapon. Beyond sieges it had very little value; in the seventeenth century artillery began to become mobile, with wheeled carriages and horse artillery, so that the guns could keep up with the movements of troops and be ready to support the infantry whenever a battle presented itself. But the mortar was, with a few exceptions, a massive and immobile piece of ordnance. Generally of cast iron and with a barrel whose wall thickness often exceeded the diameter of the bore, it sat in a ponderous wooden bed assembled from layers of timber strapped or bolted together and it was a major operation involving several men and horses and primitive rope-and-pulley hoists to dismantle the thing, get the various component parts onto wagons and transport them. Unless the enemy was co-operative enough to lock himself up in a fortress and invite a siege, there was little chance of a heavy mortar catching up with the war once it had begun.

A sixteenth-century exposition of ballistics; the mortar trajectory is divided into the 'Motus Volante' when the powder is propelling the shot; 'Motus Mixtus' when gravity is beginning to have an effect; and 'Motus Naturalis' when gravity takes complete charge. For some reason or other, gravity appears to have no effect upon the trajectory of the gun.

MORTAR GUNNERY

The mortars of this period were set into their platforms at a fixed elevation so that variation in range was achieved by altering the powder charge. The barrel was very short, no more than two or three times the calibre, and the calibre was generally quite large – larger than the average gun of the day; mortars of up to 15in calibre were quite normal. Aiming was done with nothing more than a length of string, a lead weight and a piece of chalk. Using the chalk, the gunner drew a line down the top surface of the mortar barrel on the axis of the bore. He then took the string and weight and found a position from where he could see both the mortar and the target. Holding up the string and plumb bob he lined up the string with the target. Then by hand signals, shouts and doubtless curses, he directed the remainder of his detachment to heave and prise the mortar and carriage until the plumb line, the chalk line and the target were all aligned. That took care of the direction; range was simply a matter of estimating the distance and, using the gunner's art, judging how much gunpowder would be needed to throw the projectile to land on the target. And where the target was a fortress, an error of a few score yards was not of great importance; there were plenty of things inside a fortress that would suffer if a bomb landed on them.

The only exception to the heavy siege mortar was the 'Coehorn Mortar', so-called from its originator, Baron Menno van Coehorn, a Dutch fortification engineer. He developed this small mortar firing a bomb of about 24lb (11kg) weight at the siege of Grave in 1674, which thereafter became a favourite form of portable mortar that could accompany troops in the field and be used as a bombardment weapon to deal with minor obstacles.

Mallet's Mortar

There were occasional cases of giantism, going on the theory that if a large mortar was good, a larger one would be even better. The French employed a large 'long-range' 13in mortar at the Siege of Cadiz in 1810, and a number of 24in mortars weighing 7 tons (7,000kg) were employed at the Siege of Antwerp in 1832. The nineteenth century culmination of this tendency appeared in 1857 with the 36in wrought-iron mortar designed by Mr Mallet for employment in the Crimean War.

The Siege of Sebastopol had led to a demand for a piece of heavy ordnance capable of throwing a really heavy and destructive shell. Several

British mortars at the siege of Sebastopol, 1854. Note that the central mortar is being laid by plumb line, with two men shifting it sideways by means of handspikes.

Mallet's 36in mortar; destined for the Crimea, the war ended before it was built.

designs were put forward, but the one by Mr Mallet, an Irish engineer, caught the eye of Lord Palmerston, who on 1 May 1855 minuted the Lieutenant General of the Ordnance:

I am so fully satisfied of the probable success of Mr Mallet's scheme that I am willing to take upon myself, as First Minister of the Crown, the full responsibility of carrying it into execution; and I therefore request that you will, without the slightest delay, take the necessary steps for the immediate construction of two mortars . . . time is an essential element in this matter and too much time has already been lost in needless hesitation.

Not for the first time, nor the last, a politician was about to back a loser in the military technical stakes.

Mallet's Mortar was of unusual construction, devised to withstand the high pressures that would be necessary to discharge a shell weighing approximately 1½ tons (1,525kg) – Mallet was a little unsure of the exact weight he would eventually select – and was built up from a series of component parts held together by external bracing. The basis was a cast-iron base, 30in (76cm) thick and carrying the trunnions and an anchoring ring for the external braces. Into this the chamber was formed, and the top surface was recessed for the insertion of a wrought-iron forged ring about 70in (180cm) long and with a 36in (90cm) hole in its centre. On top of this went three hoops of diminishing thickness, surmounted by a heavy muzzle hoop with a flange that fitted over the topmost barrel ring. Then there were six square-section bolts which passed through holes in the muzzle hoop and in the chamber flange and were retained by cotter pins; these wedge-like pins, driven in with sledgehammers, pulled the bolts down and compressed the various component rings to result in a gas-tight barrel about 11ft (3.5m) long and weighing some 42 tons (42,700kg).

All this sat on a cast-iron bedplate that held the trunnions, which were at the front lower edge of the mortar base. Elevation was achieved by driving in two enormous wooden 'quoins' or wedges, one from each side, between the bedplate and the underside of the base piece. There was also an 'elevating screw' which could be used to make small adjustments to the elevation once the wedges had been positioned.

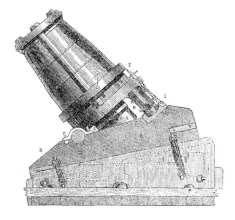

Side view of Mallet's mortar; S is the elevation adjusting screw, and D the wedge driven in beneath the rear of the mortar to give rough elevation.

A company called Mare, at Blackwall in London, tendered for the construction on 7 May 1855, quoting a price of £4,900 for each mortar, including the beds, to be delivered in ten weeks. In fact it took ninety-six weeks, and the Crimean War had been over for a year when the two mortars were finally delivered in May 1857. Mare & Co. had gone bankrupt trying to make the mortars; the job was then passed to Horsfall & Co., who made the forgings, and to Fawcett, Preston & Co., who machined them. Much of the delay had been due to flaws in the enormous forgings which only became apparent when the machining commenced.

Fifty cast-iron shells, of weights varying from 2,350 to 2,950lb (1,065–1,340kg) and capable of holding from 405 to 487lb (180–220kg) of gunpowder were also supplied, and on October 19 1857 the first firing took place. Wisely, the propelling charge was started at the safely low figure of 10lb (4.5kg), throwing a 2,370lb (1,075kg) shell to 370yd (340m); the charge was then gradually increased until by the end of the day the seventh round was a 2,550lb (1,160kg) shell launched by 70lb (30kg) of powder to reach 2,644yd (2,418m). But not without some misgivings:

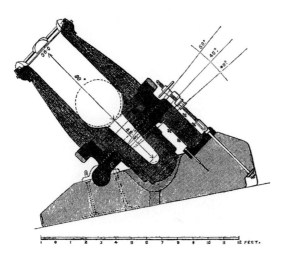

Section through Mallet's mortar showing the powder chamber.

At Round 5 it was seen that the rear retaining screw was not strong enough to resist the shock it received. At Round 7 a crack, four inches long, appeared in the second hoop of the centre ring, and the Committee, as a precaution, deemed it necessary to have the hoop removed and repaired.

The mortar was repaired, at a cost of £56, and the trial resumed in December; after six rounds the centre hoop broke once more and the joints between the various rings began to open, More repairs were authorized and carried out, with the trials recommencing in July 1858. This time the cotters holding the longitudinal bolts began to shear, and on the sixth shot one entire bolt snapped and the muzzle ring shifted. Mr Mallet confidently asked for further repairs, but by that time there was a new Secretary of State for War who had no patience with the mortar and refused to sanction the expense. The question was raised a year later after another new Secretary of State had taken office, but he referred it back to the Ordnance Select Committee, whose members stated that they could 'see no practical advantage to the public service was likely to be obtained by continuing the experiments', and that was the end. The damaged mortar was scrapped. The second mortar, which had been delivered to Woolwich Arsenal, was assembled, put on a plinth, and stayed there for many years until the Arsenal closed, whereupon it was moved to a position outside the Royal Artillery Barracks at Woolwich, where it can be seen to this day.

Coastal Mortars

The mortar remained more or less at the same state of development until the twentieth century. The British 13in mortar of the 1850s, employed as a naval weapon for shore bombardment and also as a coast defence weapon – Mohammed's original idea having been revived – was still a short and stubby cast-iron tube clamped solidly to a wooden base, with the propelling charge a

A British 13in mortar of the nineteenth century, displayed at Pendennis Castle, Cornwall. The elevation was fixed at 45 degrees and the range was varied by varying the powder charge.

Drill with a siege mortar in the 1870s. By tipping it forward onto the front edge of its bed the wheels could be removed and then the mortar and bed tipped back to rest on the ground in the firing position.

matter of guess and try by the gunner in charge. It was not until the 1860s that the idea of providing a fixed propelling charge and varying the mortar's elevation was ever considered, and this radical step was urged in an attempt to promote the mortar as a suitable weapon for attacking the decks of iron-clad warships by dropping heavy projectiles onto the less protected deck areas instead of trying to batter a way in through the thick side armour belts. This policy gained acceptance during the 1880s and the US Coast Artillery were among the foremost enthusiasts for the system, installing large numbers of 12in 'mortars' in coast fortresses all round the USA. In fact, these mortars were breech-loading rifled guns, but since they always fired at angles above 45 degrees they were rightly termed 'mortars'.

TWILIGHT OF THE SIEGE MORTAR

The final deployment of the classic siege mortar came with the sieges that occurred during the American Civil War. The 24-pounder Coehorn

Assembling a heavy mortar in the field during the American Civil War.

A Union Army mortar battery outside Petersburg in 1865.

mortar of 5.8in calibre appeared first, since it was readily portable; the American version weighed about 270lb (120kg) complete with its wooden bed, and was provided with four handles so that it could be lifted by four men and moved short distances or heaved onto a wagon for longer moves. Heavier mortars were produced once the likelihood of a prolonged war and siege operations became apparent. Both sides produced 8in, 10in and 13in mortars, and their efficiency was

such that the 13in could fire a 220lb (100kg) bomb to a range in excess of 4,000yd (3,700m).

One of the reasons that the American Civil War signalled the end of the classic siege mortar was because it also marked the appearance of breech-loading and rifled artillery. This tendency gathered pace, so much so that when the Prussian Army laid siege to the French border fortresses in 1870 there was scarcely a mortar to be seen; it was almost entirely done with breech-loading

'Dictator', a famous Union Army 13-inch mortar, preparing to bombard Richmond.

A Union mortar battery outside Yorktown in 1862.

howitzers. The Prusso-Danish and Prusso-Austrian wars of the 1860s had been fought with a mixture of old and new artillery deployed in accordance with age-old tactical ideas, and the artillery did not emerge from them with much credit. From 1866 to 1870 a radical overhaul of Prussian artillery equipment and tactics took place, which led to the artillery being at the forefront of the battle line in 1870.

However, at the same time, the infantry had been strengthened by the adoption of breech-loading rifles, and for a while in the 1870s the situation arose where the infantryman's rifle had a better range than some artillerymen's guns, which made the forefront of the line a hazardous place for artillery.

MORTARS FOR THE INFANTRY?

The German army appears to have been the first to see the need for a lightweight piece of siege

Probably the first railway-mounted ordnance was this 13-inch mortar, also used in the siege of Richmond.

artillery which infantry could use to deal with minor strong points without the need to call up heavier 'artillery of position', and after various trials and proposals the army developed its first minenwerfer in about 1908. This was a simple smooth-bore steel tube on a wooden base and capable of being carried by two men. A metal framework allowed the barrel to be clamped at a number of different angles of elevation, but, strangely enough, the maximum angle was no more than 25 degrees, which somewhat negates any claim to the weapon being called a mortar; nevertheless, the intention was clear enough. A small cast-iron bomb with an impact fuze was breech-loaded with a gunpowder charge composed of a number of small bags, so that the amount of charge could be varied to give a number of range options for each fixed elevation. Fired by a simple percussion-cap arrangement, the bomb was hurled into the air and dropped a few hundred yards away; thus a short, sharp bombardment could be kept up by the two-man team operating the weapon, so as to give an enemy strongpoint a softening up before the infantry went into the assault.

A more carefree arrangement, which fore-shadowed some of the apparatus to be seen in the following years, was noted in the *Kriegstechnische*

Zeitschrifte, a German military periodical, for January 1914. After referring to Japanese use of the hand grenade at Port Arthur, it observed that such devices might be much more effective if thrown to longer range, and noted:

> The following apparatus was developed by the Austrian Lieutenant Burstyn. The barrel is made of sheet iron, large enough in the bore to take an ordinary cylindrical tin can. Three rifles, with their barrels sawn off short, are fixed into the breech end with their butts up against a rubber pad clamped to the wooden bed. The bullets having been removed previously, the three rifles are fired simultaneously with a lanyard, thus propelling the grenade. The apparatus can be easily and cheaply extemporized in the field.

There is no record of anyone in the Austro-Hungarian Army ever 'extemporizing' this 'in the field', however. The problem of firing three rifles simultaneously must have been enough to deter any experimenter, since even a fraction of a second between the three discharges would have led to some very peculiar results. (Gunther Burstyn, the weapon's creator, was, incidentally, a man with an inventive turn of mind; he had already made an appearance in the same journal

17cm Minenwerfer

Calibre	170mm (6.6in)
Barrel length	n/a
Weight in action	520kg (1,146lb)
Elevation	45 to 75 degrees
Weight of bomb	34.5kg (76lb) (gas); 49.5kg (109lb) (HE)
Muzzle velocity	n/a
Minimum range	200m (219yd)
Maximum range	1,250m (1,368yd) (HE); 1,600m (1,750yd) (gas)

The original short 17cm minenwerfer ready for movement, with the wheels attached to the bedplate.

The 17cm medium minenwerfer was a somewhat luxurious production that resembled a shrunken siege howitzer. It had been designed before 1914, at a time when refinement and reliability came before speed of manufacture; even so, its power and robustness were sufficient to keep it in production until 1918. As can be seen from the photographs, the mortar consisted of a short barrel carried in a tubular cradle with hydrospring recoil cylinders above and below. The cradle was trunnioned into a simple triangular mounting which, in turn, was pivoted on a steel bedplate. A handwheel at the rear of the mounting drove a gear that engaged in a rack on the bedplate to traverse the mortar, and the left side of the cradle carried a very prominent elevating arc which was driven by a worm-wheel and handle at the left side of the mounting.

The barrel was rifled with six wide grooves, and the projectile was fitted with a driving band pre-engraved to fit. The powder charge was dropped into the bore, the bomb was loaded by fitting the driving band into the

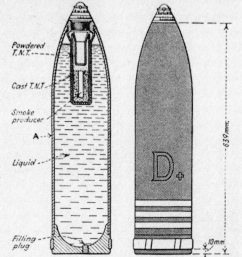

A typical 17cm projectile; this is the phosgene gas 'D-Mine'.

The longer-barrelled 17cm minenwerfer ready for action; note that the bedplate is shaped into spades on the undersurface so as to resist movement.

Minenwerfers were popular as war trophies and a few have survived. This one, in Australia, shows the hole in the breech end for the friction igniter.

rifling and ramming the bomb down on to the powder, and a friction igniter was inserted into a vent at the rear of the barrel. A lanyard was attached to the igniter and the detachment then stood clear and the mortar was fired.

The bedplate was provided with a stub axle on each side, to which wooden 'artillery' wheels could be attached, and shafts or a towing bar could be fixed to the plate for either horse-draught or manpower.

The original version had a very short barrel and a maximum range with the HE bomb of only 960yd (880m); by 1916 a longer-barrelled version appeared which improved the range to the figures given above.

some two years previously with a design for a track-laying military vehicle armed with light cannon and machine guns, one of the earliest recorded proposals for a tank. Although offered to both the Austro-Hungarian and German armies, the idea was not accepted.)

As can be imagined, while the German minenwerfer was a practical proposition, it was scarcely the elegant, superbly engineered and complicated sort of equipment which the pre-1914 armies adored. The drawing office of the Rheinische Metallwaren und Munitionsfabrik

therefore set about producing a 17cm minen-werfer. This looked like a shrunken siege howitzer, was a breech-loader with a hydrospring recoil system and a wheeled carriage, and was as elegant and complicated as anyone could wish for. Accepted for service early in 1914, it became the heavy minenwerfer, while the earlier model became the medium. Whether there were plans for an eventual light model is unclear; as it was, events moved rather rapidly in the summer of 1914 and the designers never had a chance to complete their programme.

2 The Coast Defence Mortar

Over the centuries, the original reason for inventing the mortar – to attack a ship from above – had been lost sight of. It seemed to be a complicated and difficult way of going about things when a simple shot from a cannon could plough through the wooden walls of contemporary ships and do all the damage that was necessary. However, the 1860s saw a sudden check to the apparent superiority of the cannon; the ironclad warship appeared.

The French opened the bidding when they began building *La Gloire* in 1858, which then naturally spurred the British, who laid down the *Warrior* in 1859. Neither of these ships was entirely of iron; they were built of wood in much the same fashion as their forebears, but were then given an outer skin of 'armour' – actually no more than a several-inch thickness of wrought iron. After a good deal of testing and trying, the Royal Navy finally settled upon a hull which consisted of 24in (60cm) of wrought iron backed by 18in (45cm) of teak wood. This proved to be the best combination for stopping shot: the wrought iron gave a hard surface for the shot to waste its energy upon, while the teak wood backing acted as a shock absorber, allowing the metal to give a little, which was a further impediment to penetration by the shot. This became known as the 'Warrior Target' and was the combination that future guns and shot would have to beat.

This, of course, meant that naval and coast defence guns, both of which had the same target in mind, would have to be a good deal more powerful than the smooth-bore 32- and 64-pounders which were generally in use. An orgy of gun design began in the late 1860s which was to lead to such muzzle-loading monsters as the 12.5in 'Woolwich Infant', and the famous 17.72in 'Hundred Ton Guns', capable of defeating up to 28in (70cm) of iron backed by 2ft of teak at over 1-mile range.

LEFROY'S MORTAR

Such giant guns were costly; they also demanded expensive mountings and large emplacements, and the problem of aiming them and obtaining accuracy at long ranges was enormous. However, in 1861 Col Lefroy of the Royal Artillery put forward a proposal to use mortars to attack warships. His argument was very simple and unanswerable: the sides of warships were getting thicker and harder every year; but the decks were neither thick nor hard; so why not drop the shot down onto the thin deck? With luck, it would go straight through the vessel and out the bottom, leaving it with a mortal wound.

Lefroy's opponents were quick to point out that the contemporary 13in Land Service mortar, a stubby device used for shelling besieged fortresses, was by no means sufficiently accurate to guarantee landing a shell in the same ocean, let alone on top of a warship. They pointed to various accuracy trials which had been conducted in the past, always with dismal results. Nevertheless, the Ordnance Select Committee was sufficiently impressed by Lefroy's argument to order a battery of twenty-one 13in mortars to be built at Puckpool, on the Isle of Wight, to command part of the Solent and protect the approaches to Portsmouth.

Trials and Tribulations

While this was still in the excavation stage, in 1863 the Committee organized yet another trial with the 13in mortar, this time to see what result it would produce when fired against the Warrior Target. (One is inclined to wonder what the Committee had in mind, since Lefroy's idea was to evade the thick sides, not to attack them directly.) In the event, the report on the trial was far from reassuring:

> As an experiment to ascertain whether, in the absence of suitable guns, mortars could be used with advantage against iron-plated ships, the Committee consider that the results obtained are not sufficiently encouraging to warrant their being so employed. The effect they produce is not serious ... and their fire is so extremely inaccurate that no reliance can be placed on their striking a target even at the limited range of 200 yards.

While Lefroy and his supporters were not slow to point out that their object was not to attack the sides of ships, they found it difficult to argue against the charge of inaccuracy. However, their hand was strengthened by a report from Capt Cooper Key, a respected gunnery expert and commander of the naval gunnery establishment HMS *Excellent*. He reported on a most successful trial with a 13in Sea Service mortar (virtually the same weapon as the Land Service pattern) at varying ranges up to 1,800 yd (1,650m), leading to the conclusion that 'vessels could not remain at anchor under the fire of mortars unless their upper decks were rendered proof against shells.' This did not stop the debate, but it was sufficient to persuade the Ordnance Select Committee to revise their opinion and increase the number of mortars at Puckpool to thirty-six.

A tactic was now formulated. Since it was difficult, if not impossible, to guarantee hitting a target with single shots, mortars would be employed in groups, and they would be sited so as to cover stretches of water into which an enemy fleet might sail and take up position to bombard some naval establishment, such as Portsmouth Dockyard, but out of range of any direct-fire guns. Should such a fleet appear, then the cluster of mortars would open fire and, by the law of averages, some of the projectiles would be bound to hit one or other of the enemy sooner or later. Even if these mortars did not sink any enemy ships, they could make life so difficult that the enemy would weigh anchor and try to find another position.

The battery at Puckpool was eventually built and, by 1870, was armed with thirty mortars and four 12in rifled muzzle loading guns, but very little other building of mortar batteries ever took place in British coast defences. Quite simply, the critics were right; it was too much expense and trouble for a very doubtful result, and to have had any real effect it would have had to be repeated every few miles around all British naval bases or important commercial ports.

A FRESH APPROACH

There the matter rested for some years, until in 1884 the Inspector General of Fortifications suddenly suggested elevating one of the now-obsolete 9in rifled muzzle loading (RML) guns to about 70 degrees and firing it as a form of mortar. With rifling and the better ballistic shape of the pointed shell, the results might well be more accurate than the old smooth-bore, short-range mortar, and there might also be a considerable economic advantage if some of the old RML guns could be given a second lease of life.

He was supported by the Superintendent of the Royal Gun Factory, who suggested that the 9in RML, as it stood, with three deep rifling grooves, would not be particularly accurate in the mortar role, but that he would be happy to re-line one and cut fresh polygroove rifling for the purpose of a trial. The Superintendent of the Royal Carriage Department then weighed in with a proposed modification to the gun carriage to permit high elevation, following which the Ordnance Select Committee gave the project its blessing, and by December 1884 a gun had been prepared and a trial was fired at the School of Gunnery at Shoeburyness in Essex.

To general astonishment, the weapon proved capable of very accurate fire to a range of 10,000yd (9,150m). After pondering this, the Ordnance Select Committee suggested boring out and re-lining another gun, but this time to 10in calibre, and repeating the trial, the larger shell promising even better ballistics and a better effect at the target. Everybody concurred, the necessary work was put in hand, and in 1885 a comparative trial of the two guns, 9in and 10in, was arranged.

The trial showed that the 10in was indeed superior, both in accuracy and in target effect.

Now came the acid test; put a high-angle gun into a service fort and try it against real targets. In February 1886 orders were given for a 10in gun to be installed at Warden Point Fort on the Isle of Wight, and the next three years were spent in conducting firing trials against towed targets and devising a suitable fire-control system. Finally, in 1890, the whole question was examined, reports of all the tests and trials were studied, and the decision taken to install high-angle batteries at

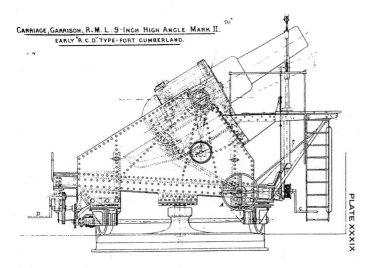

CARRIAGE, GARRISON, R.M.L. 9-INCH HIGH ANGLE MARK II.
EARLY "R.C.D." TYPE - FORT CUMBERLAND.

PLATE XXXIX

The first British design for a coast defence mortar was this version, used in Steynewood Battery on the Isle of Wight in 1889 and moved to Fort Cumberland at Portsmouth in 1899.

Taking an entirely new look at the idea, this was to replace the Mark 1 pattern. The gunner is turning the elevating wheel, which rotates around a screwed rod attached to the mortar and so pulls on the breech to elevate the muzzle.

Unfortunately, as can just be seen here, the screwed rod came so far out that it fouled the side wall of the gun pit. Design rejected.

various places throughout the Empire where is seemed probable than an enemy fleet might take up a bombardment position out of reach of direct-fire guns.

Anticlimax

In fact, relatively few of these early mortars were ever built. It is impossible to find any documentary evidence, but there certainly seems to have been a lack of enthusiasm for this type of weapon in British service. Between 1890, when the decision was taken, and 1930 when the last 'high-angle guns' were finally declared obsolete and removed from service, no more than ten batteries were built. High-angle guns were installed as follows:

9in High Angle	Number	Date
Steynewood Bty, IoW	6	1889
Quarry Bty, Portland	6	1890
Tregantle Down Bty, Plymouth	4	1890
Rame Church Bty, Plymouth	4	1893
Hawkins Bty, Plymouth	4	1898
Fort Cumberland, Portsmouth	2	1899
10in High Angle		
Ghargur HA Bty, Malta	6	1899
Spyglass Bty, Gibraltar	6	1899–
Middle Hill Bty, Gibraltar	6	1900–
Wongneichong Gap Bty, Hong Kong	1	1901

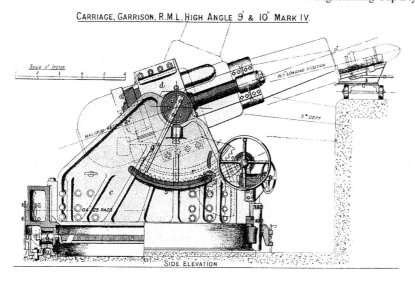

CARRIAGE, GARRISON, R.M.L. HIGH ANGLE 9" & 10" MARK IV.

The final design used a more conventional method of elevating. Note the muzzle-loading trolley on the parapet wall.

Most of these guns remained in place until the early 1920s and were then removed; three batteries had their RMLs taken out in the early 1900s and replaced by 9.2in breech-loading high-angle guns:

9.2in BL Mk VI High Angle	Number	Date
Rame Church Bty, Plymouth	2	1906
Wongneichong Gap Bty, Hong Kong	1	1908
Hawkins Bty, Plymouth	2	1914

These batteries remained in service until the late 1920s, the last guns being withdrawn in 1930. And that, as far as the British Army is concerned, is the story of the high-angle coast defence mortar.

COLONEL ABBOT'S MORTARS

It was a different story in the USA. An officer in the Corps of Engineers, Lt Col H.L. Abbot, had commanded a battery of Volunteer Artillery at the Siege of St Petersburg, during the American Civil War. There he had seen mortars, of both sides, in action, and he came to the conclusion that the only worthwhile way to use mortars was to collect a number of them together and fire them in a salvo so as to blanket the target area. When the mortar discussion appeared in print from Britain, Abbott recollected his wartime thoughts and proposed a sea-coast battery of sixteen mortars arranged as four mortars in each of four pits, the centres of the pits being the four corners of a rectangle. This, he contended, would produce a shot pattern which would cover any warship and virtually guarantee that at least one and probably more shells would hit the target.

In 1874 Abbott actually built a battery at Willett's Point, New York, but it was never armed, and the matter rested until 1885 when, after a certain amount of national debate over the state of the US defences, President Grover Cleveland convened a Board of Inquiry under Secretary of War William C. Endicott.

THE ENDICOTT BOARD

The Endicott Board laid down the foundations of American coast defence for the rest of its days, but the significant point here is that among the Board members was none other than General (as he now was) Abbott, who lost little time in promoting his views on coastal mortars. They were accepted and formed part of the Board's recommendations; work began on a suitable weapon, and the first mortar battery was built at Fort Winfield Scott in the Predidio of San Francisco in 1894–5; four others were also begun at Forts Slocum and Hancock, New York, Fort Banks, Boston and Fort Moultrie, Charleston. All were built to the same pattern as previously envisaged by Abbott, four mortars in a rectangular pit about 50ft square, and four pits arranged in a square. The ammunition magazines were behind the pit walls, protected by several feet of earth and layers of concrete. Each mortar was a breech-loading 12in calibre rifled gun, mounted on a turntable and capable of firing at elevations between 45 and 80 degrees. And above and behind the pits, or off to a flank, depending upon the lie of the land, was the observing station from which fire could be controlled. The essential point of the layout was that the mortars were completely invisible from the sea, being well below ground level.

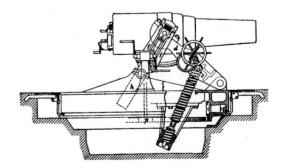

The design fundamentals of the American coast mortars; big springs and an hydraulic shock absorber in the cylinder marked 'h'.

British construction of coastal mortars was rather less involved, relying more upon finding a suitable piece of ground so that the guns could be concealed behind a natural crest. But in both cases, the concealment was short-lived; as soon as the guns fired their first shots a pall of smoke would reveal their position. But this was not really a serious drawback, since no warship in existence had guns which could have dropped shells into the mortar pits except at ranges at which the mortars would never have engaged them anyway.

These batteries were the test bed for Abbott's theories of engagement, and some fundamental defects soon became apparent. Abbott had ruled that all mortars would fire at once, all parallel, their direction being the bearing from the centre of the four pits to the centre of the target. Since

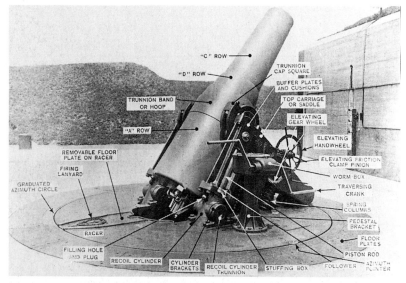

How it looked in the textbooks, complete with explanation. A 12in M1890 on Carriage M1896.

How it looked in real life; four 12in mortars of Fort Taylor, Florida, preparing to fire. This picture shows the massive concrete structure of the pit, and it is easy to imagine how the blast would reflect off these surfaces.

The salvo is fired – and a shell caught in flight. The gunners in the foreground appear nonchalant, but doubtless their ears were ringing.

And now the free-for-all as four gun detachments struggle to reload without getting in each other's way.

the average error of any one mortar was, in those days, quite large, firing all sixteen at once gave some assurance that the target would be struck by one or two shots from each salvo, and since the shells weighed around three-quarters of a ton, a couple of hits would do quite satisfactory damage. However, while all this was quite true, what Abbott had failed to foresee was the effect on the gunners of firing four 12in mortars at the same time in a concrete pit; the blast was fearful, and caused the evacuation of all the air in the pit, immediately followed by a wave of pressure as the air flowed back, leaving the gunners lightly concussed and damaging lights and other fitments in the pit. And if the doors to the magazines and storerooms were left open the blast entered these and blew the doors off their hinges and created all sorts of havoc. It also transpired that there was simply not enough room for four gun detachments to load their guns all at the same time without bumping into one another; trolleys with heavy shells were being trundled through, rammers with long staves being waved about, and chaos reigned.

Improvements to the System

By the time these drawbacks had been identified (lack of funds prevented firing these batteries more than once or twice a year), there had been some improvements in the design of the mountings and of the guns themselves, both of which contributed to improved accuracy and speed of loading. As a result, the first question raised was whether the sixteen mortars should be fired parallel and all at the same point, or whether each pit should be permitted to fire on its own data determined from its own centre. We need not delve into the mathematics, but it can be shown that if the probable error of the falling shell is smaller than the rectangle of the pit, then firing in parallel actually reduces the chances of a hit.

Some experimental firings proved the validity of this argument, whereupon the reason for grouping the four pits in a square vanished completely, and henceforth it was possible to place the pits in the most convenient positions according to the terrain being occupied.

The next batch of mortar batteries, the building of which began in 1896, was therefore built with all four pits in a line; these pits were three-sided, the rear being left open, so that the effect of the blast was no longer confined and life became more tolerable for the gunners. However, the drawback in this arrangement was that the magazines and store galleries were now in front of the mortars, in the forward parapet, and the damage from the muzzle blast entering these galleries was dangerous.

A new tactic also now evolved; instead of firing all sixteen mortars at once, while each pit would still fire its four mortars at once the pits would fire at intervals, one after the other. By choosing a suitable interval, such as thirty or forty-five seconds, by the time the interval after the fourth pit had passed, the first was ready to fire again, and so a constant bombardment could be kept up. Under the old system there had been a roar of sixteen mortars firing and then nothing for five or six minutes before the next salvo could be fired.

The next query to arise was whether sixteen shells were actually needed; with gradual

Maintenance on a 12in Mortar M1908 in the defences of San Francisco.

The 12in mortar M1912 was the last design to be produced, and numbers were taken from the coast defences and mounted on railway trucks in World War I. They remained in use well into World War II.

improvements in the mortar and its mounting, the rate of fire was improving; perhaps two four-mortar pits firing alternately might be just as effective at the target as four pits? This was tried and shown to be correct, and from 1897 onwards mortar batteries consisted of two four-mortar pits. The rate of fire was now in the order of one round per minute, instead of the one round every five or six minutes of the original mortars of 1890.

The last modification was due to improvements in observation, range-finding and fire control, which improved the accuracy and reduced the probable error. This led to the practice (originally on economy grounds) of firing only two of the mortars in each pit, and it was soon appreciated that fewer men in the pit during reloading meant less congestion and a faster rate of fire. The pits still had four mortars in them, but only two were now fired together.

CONSOLIDATION AND MODERNIZATION

This was the final form of the mortar battery in US service, though there were still improvements in the weapons. The 12in mortar had progressed from the M1885 to the M1912, and by that time the Ordnance Department was contemplating something heavier, such as a 14in mortar, as well as actually building and testing a longer (20 calibre) 12in design. But all this was swept aside in 1915 when, after observing the course of the war in Europe, the US Coast Artillery and the Ordnance Department decided on a radical overhaul of the defences. The war had shown that modern warships with improved weapons and fire control could sit out at sea and out-range most American batteries (whether the ships could have *hit* them at that range is a question that does not appear to have been addressed). There would, therefore, be a modernization of US Coast batteries with fourteen new batteries of very powerful 16in guns. And to supplement these direct-fire weapons there would be sixty new 16in 'howitzers' – a name chosen to distinguish these new long-barrelled models from the older stubby-barrelled mortars. These would equip two mortar batteries in support of each 16in gun battery

This programme would obviously take several years to put into effect; neither 16in guns nor their mountings are built overnight. But before the programme had got into its stride the USA was drawn into the World War. Although there were demands for every kind of munition, the coast defence programme survived and even prospered, resulting in the construction of specimens of both the 16in gun and the 16in howitzer. But quantity production had to wait for a new gun factory, dedicated to production of 14in and 16in weapons for both the army and the navy, to be built on Neville Island on the Ohio river, near Pittsburg. However, as with so many of the long-term projects initiated in the USA in 1917, this was ended before any production could begin and the project was abandoned early in 1919. Four howitzers were built by Watervliet Arsenal and they were emplaced as Battery Pennington at Fort Story, guarding the entrance to Chesapeake Bay. This signalled the end of mortar development in

US coast defences, because in the wake of World War I there was no money to be spared for military construction throughout the 1920s and early 1930s, and when World War II began to loom, the only coast defences to receive any funding were the long-promised 16in gun batteries.

ACTION AT LAST

It showed be noted, however, that the American 12in mortars did rank among the few coast defence weapons which actually fired on an enemy. Two mortar batteries formed part of the considerable armament of Fort Mills on Corregidor Island: Battery Way with four 12in mortars in a single pit and Battery Geary with eight 12in mortars in two pits. During the Japanese siege of Corregidor these two batteries fired onto the Bataan Peninsula and did considerable damage, though they were, of course, firing anti-ship projectiles rather than anti-personnel shells. But they soon became the target of Japanese retaliatory fire from their ten 240mm howitzers deployed on Bataan and also from daily air raids. The most telling blow came from the howitzer fire; Japanese concrete-piercing shells soon wrecked two of the mortars of Battery Way, and Battery Geary was totally destroyed when a shell pierced the cover and

End of an era: one of the mortars of Battery Geary on Corregidor Island, shattered by the explosion of the magazine under Japanese bombardment. Photograph taken after the recapture of the island by US troops in 1945.

entered the magazine located in the dividing mound between the two pits. The shell detonated the contents of the magazine, and the explosion, heard all over the island, blew slabs of concrete over huge distances and threw the mortars and their mountings around like toys.

France used mortars to protect the mouth of the Gironde and other important targets, Germany to protect the Kiel Canal and the Elbe, and Japan went to the extent of building an artificial island in the middle of Tokyo Bay to mount a sizeable battery of mortars. The Japanese were particularly fond of mortars and had no less than 133 emplaced around the shores of Japan, as well as several hundred guns. But they deserve a special mention for the innovative use of coast defence mortars which brought a completely new force to the battlefield.

FROM COAST TO FIELD

In 1894–5 the first Sino-Japanese War took place, and among the major actions was the Japanese capture of the fortified Chinese port of Ta-Lien-Wan. This involved a brief bombardment and assault of some minor defences and was all over in an hour or two. But the Japanese were not allowed to keep their spoils, and within a very short time Ta-Lien-Wan had come under Russian ownership and was called Port Arthur. It was then given some powerful fortifications designed by none other than Todleben, the fortress engineer who had so brilliantly held off the Allies at Sebastopol.

In the event, Todleben's designs were incompetently carried out and the defences were never properly completed before the Japanese attacked the place in 1904, thus initiating the Russo-Japanese War. Shortly after that the place was besieged, but this time there was to be no walkover for the Japanese.

Nor were they expecting one; they had watched the fortification process and knew that even though the defences were incomplete, they were going to have a very tough target; so they made their plans. And no sooner had the siege lines been drawn up across the Kwantung Peninsula, isolating Port Arthur from the rest of Manchuria, than engineers were at work dismantling heavy 28cm (11in) coast mortars protecting Japanese naval installations. These were laboriously dragged to the docks, loaded aboard ship and set sail for Korea. And in one of the rare Russian

One of the Japanese 28cm coast mortars transplanted into the Siege of Port Arthur in 1904. Batteries of these mortars were dragged into position by hundreds of men using ropes and rollers.

successes of the war, the transport ran into a Russian patrolling warship and was sunk, complete with its cargo.

More mortars were dismantled, shipped and landed successfully on the Manchurian mainland. They were then manhandled, by hundreds of labourers, on rollers and with ropes and pulleys, into the siege lines around Port Arthur, and after being reassembled they opened fire on the Russian Far Eastern Fleet cowering inside the harbour, effectively putting it out of action with a few score shells. They then turned their attention to the fortifications and began systematically battering them. Port Arthur fell, and the Japanese carted their mortars back home and re-emplaced them in their original locations.

In Europe, every border was fortified to a greater or lesser degree, and any country contemplating moving beyond its own borders knew it would have to confront steel and concrete. But there was one near-constant factor in all European land fortification: the constructors knew that they could never be attacked with any artillery of greater calibre than 24cm (9.45in), because that was the largest piece of artillery that could be moved by animal power. And there was

nothing else available to move guns when those forts were designed. Even a 24cm weapon had to be reduced to its basic parts and loaded onto several wagons before it could move, and it then took several days to put back together again when it arrived wherever it was needed.

Consequently, the fortress engineers built their forts to withstand 24cm howitzer shells; or if possible, as an insurance policy, to withstand 28cm shells. Now the Japanese were suddenly employing a 28cm mortar on a land battlefield. Krupp, the famous German gunmaker, took note. He had recently built a rather good 42cm (16.5in) mortar for coast defence, and having observed the Japanese performance he now redesigned it to be capable of rapid dismantling, using a small travelling crane, and transportation on specially built railway trucks. He offered this to the German Army.

The German Army, not unreasonably, thanked Herr Krupp but pointed out that the railways did not always go where the guns were wanted, and that something of the same size but road-mobile would be a more practical weapon. Krupp returned to his drawing board and presently came back with a smaller weapon, though still of the

The Italians took the idea from the Japanese in 1916 and sent some of their 30.5cm coast mortars into the Alps to bombard Austrian positions that normal guns could not reach.

The 42cm 'Gamma' mortar developed by Krupp as a powerful coast defence weapon and which fathered 'Big Bertha'.

Rear view of 'Gamma' showing the breech open and a round of ammunition on a trolley. The sloping structure beyond the trolley was an elevator for lifting the ammunition to the breech platform.

The Austro-Hungarian empire had a coastline in the Adriatic and the Skoda company built these 30.5cm mortars to defend it. As with the Krupp design, they could be placed on transport wagons and in 1914 became siege mortars.

same 42cm calibre, which could be stripped into no more than five loads and towed by Daimler-Benz petrol-driven tractors. The Army was suitably impressed, and bought two mortars, formed them into Kurz Marine Kanone Batterie 3, and in August 1914 set out for Liège and its ring of forts. The weapons were officially called the 42cm Mörser L/14; the troops called them 'Big Bertha'. In three days of leisurely firing their 1,800lb (820kg) shells the two mortars totally silenced the twelve forts surrounding Liège, destroying two of them beyond any possible repair and severely damaging some of the others. Thanks to the Japanese example, the Germans had initiated an entirely new phase in siege warfare and had demonstrated, in a very practical manner, that the age of fortification was coming to its close.

3 The Trench Mortar

When the 1914–18 War began, the German army possessed 116 medium and 44 heavy minenwerfers, which were held and operated by the Pioneer companies of infantry regiments. They saw little employment initially until the war reached its static phase, but by late 1914 they were in common use. At the same time another weapon arrived in the form of the Krupp Trench Howitzer, which was the first of a class of weapon which came to be known as the 'Toffee-Apple Mortars' from the odd form of their projectiles.

The Krupp mortar had been privately developed in 1912, but had not been accepted by the army at that time. It was a smooth-bore of about 2in (50mm) calibre, mounted on a wooden bed which could be trundled about on two wheels. The wheels could then be removed to place the weapon in action. The barrel had a range of elevation from 45 to 80 degrees, and the projectile was a thin-walled spherical bomb on top of a 2in-calibre stalk. The stalk was loaded into the barrel

Moving the Krupp Trench Howitzer was simply a matter of putting wheels on the two stub axles and handles into brackets on the mortar bed.

of the mortar, over a small charge of smokeless powder, and the 187lb (85kg) bomb could be fired to a maximum range of 350yd (320m). Being a thin-cased weapon it had a considerable blast and disruptive effect at the target. The stick remained on the bomb in flight and helped to stabilize it so that it landed on its nose to detonate by means of a simple impact fuze.

The appearance of these weapons along the Front Line led to cries from the British and French troops, who demanded some form of retaliatory weapon. The British had, in fact, known about the minenwerfer before the war broke out and had asked their designers for some sort of similar weapon, but other things had greater priority and nothing much had been done. But when the complaints started arriving in November 1914, action was taken in the easiest possible manner; a captured German minenwerfer was sent to Woolwich and a hundred copies were rapidly turned out and sent to France by Christmas of 1914 in order to satisfy the troops until something better could be produced. Gunmakers and engineering companies were informed of the requirement and the army waited to see what would turn up.

A contemporary picture showing the Krupp Trench Howitzer and its 'Toffee Apple' bomb in the firing position. Note the stub axle sticking out of the side, beneath the vertical sight bracket.

German handbook picture showing the principal features of their light minenwerfer:

1. Barrel
2. Breechblock with handle
3. Firing mechanism
4. Clinometer plane
5. Elevation scale
6. Elevation lever
7. Elevation locking wheel
8. Stand
9. Barrel ring
10. Ground platform
11. Barrel brush
12. Box for accessories
13. Carrying handles
14. Bolt anchoring gun mount to platform.

THE SUICIDE CLUB

What turned up was the weirdest collection of ironmongery ever to grace anybody's battlefield. Impressed with the need to make the new weapon cheap and simple, the various inventors succeeded only in producing designs which were so primitive as to defy description. In addition, the storekeepers in France had dug into odd corners and actually resurrected some old cast-iron and bronze mortars dating from the middle of the previous century, together with a stock of bombs, and had dispatched them to the Front to form the initial armament of the new 'Trench Mortar Service'. This was less formally known as the 'Suicide Club' and was officially born on 26 November 1914 at Pont du Hem, near Estaires, being composed of two British officers and nine gunners of the Royal Horse and Royal Garrison Artillery. The weapons they received astonished them: two 6in mortars, one cast at Breguet in 1848 and one at Toulouse in 1842, both of which had, they were assured, served with distinction in the Crimea. These were later augmented by an 8in of equal antiquity. The projectiles were cast-iron spherical shells, also of Crimean

vintage, and the propelling charge was loose gunpowder, poured into the chamber before inserting the shell. Firing was performed by inserting an electric mining detonator through the vent and firing it, from a safe distance, with an electric dynamo.

To quote one of the members of the original Suicide Club, 'The mortar was then collected from wherever it had come to rest, cleaned, sometimes a little work with a brace and bit was necessary to clear the vent, and the performance repeated.' A variation was to load the mortar with a wooden block of the correct calibre which filled the barrel to the muzzle and then, on top of the block, balance the next larger calibre of bomb, wedging it in place with bricks and wood until it was fired. Using the correct calibre of bomb these weapons could range to about 300yd (275m); the oversized bomb could manage about 80yd (70m). These relics were used with some trepidation until the arrival of some official British patterns early in 1915. The British Fourth Army had already begun constructing its own mortars from water-pipe, manufacturing tin-can bombs filled with mining explosives to use as projectiles, in order to supplement the French antiques, and

33

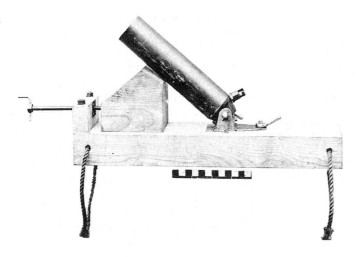

The British 4in rifled muzzle-loading mortar of 1915, surely the most basic and primitive piece of ordnance of the twentieth century.

By comparison with the 4in RML mortar, the 4in smooth-bore was a positively sophisticated weapon.

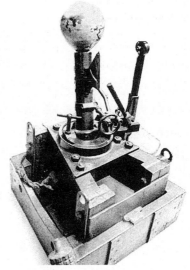

As might be expected from Vickers, their version of the Krupp howitzer was a much more luxurious production. The vertical stalk on the right side is the sight bracket.

shortly after this the Second Army opened a foundry at Armentières which cast 3.7in mortars from scrap brass cartridge cases. Units were provided with these mortars in exchange for an equivalent weight of empty cartridge cases so that production was more or less self-sustaining.

The first weapon to appear in the line with a really official backing was a rifled muzzle-loading 4in constructed at Woolwich Arsenal by boring out and rifling naval armour-piercing 6in (152mm) shells which had failed to pass proof. The nose of the shell was anchored into a wooden

baseplate, the rear end becoming the muzzle of the mortar, the barrel was supported, and elevation applied, by a wooden wedge operated by a screwed rod with a handle at the front. The shell was made with two rows of studs to take the rifling, an interesting regression to the rifled muzzle-loading guns of fifty years previously. The bombs weighed about 8lb (4kg) and were fired by a guncotton charge ignited by a cut-down rifle mechanism locked into a bayonet-jointed vent in the rear of the barrel. With a range of some 900yd (820m), these rifled mortars were well-received and quite effective, and remained in use in considerable numbers until they were superseded by the Stokes pattern in 1916. Indeed, some appear to have stayed in use throughout the war, since both the mortar and its ammunition were not declared obsolete until 1920.

Another issue design, though appearing in lesser numbers, was a smooth-bore 4in which was simply a length of commercial steel tube welded to a steel baseplate; the barrel was supported by a simple bipod with an even simpler screwed rod giving the required elevation. The projectile was devoid of any form of stabilization, and the fuzing was the usual length of safety fuze lit by the flash of the propelling charge. These were less successful than the rifled model, large numbers of them bursting within a few days of being taken

into use, probably because the barrel was a good deal less robust than the ex-armour piercing shell pattern of the rifled weapon.

The variety of designs proposed was endless: one is forced to the conclusion that if these were the accepted models, then the ones which were turned down must have been an odd lot. Vickers, the prominent armament manufacturers, produced their equivalent of the Krupp Trench Howitzer in their 40mm (1.57in) mortar, known by the troops as the 'Football on a Stick' or the 'Toffee-Apple Mortar' from the shape of the projectile. It fired a stick-mounted spherical bomb, similar to that of the Krupp weapon but lighter in weight and thus achieving a better range. They had also offered a design based upon their pre-war 75mm mountain howitzer, but it was felt that this, with breech-loading and a recoil system, was too much of a mechanical complication, would be too cumbersome to be conveniently handled in a trench, and would be too difficult to produce in the time and quantities demanded, so it was turned down.

Firing the Vickers 1.57in Trench Howitzer. Notice that the sight and bracket have been removed prior to firing, a standard practice with many mortars right into the 1940s.

2in TH Mk 1

2in Trench Howitzer Mark 1

Calibre	2.0in (51mm)
Barrel length	36.1in (917mm)
Weight in action	105lb (47.6kg)
Elevation	+45 degrees to +76.5 degrees
Weight of bomb	60lb (27.2kg)
Muzzle velocity	250 ft/sec (76m/sec)
Minimum range	100yd (91m)
Maximum range	500yd (457m)

The Vickers 2in trench howitzer (TH) was another of the 'Toffee-Apple Mortars', so-called because of the oversized spherical bomb they fired. The first of this class in British service was the 1.57in mortar, which was more or less copied from a pre-war Krupp design. It was then improved into a more simple pattern by Vickers, entered service late in 1915 and continued in use until 1918. Although technically overtaken by the Stokes designs, the fact remained that it was a simple, cheap and easily portable mortar which threw a 60lb (27kg) bomb and did a great deal of damage.

The barrel was a 3ft (90cm) drawn-steel tube pinned into a simple bracket attached to the wooden bed. At the front of the bed was an elevation screw to which the upper part of the barrel was attached and which also had a limited amount of traverse provided for fine adjustment. Larger adjustments were simply a matter of heaving the wooden bed in the required direction. The propelling charge was in three portions, allowing some degree of range adjustment, and was loaded into the mortar from the muzzle. The stick bomb was then loaded, the 2in diameter stick being thrust into the barrel and extending about halfway down. The spherical bomb, or warhead, was tight against the muzzle. Firing was done by inserting a friction igniter into a vent in the base of the barrel and firing it by means of a lanyard. Half of the barrel acted as the chamber, allowing the propelling gas to expand and accelerate the bomb relatively gently. The stick acted as a stabilizer and ensured that the bomb landed on its fuze, though some were fired with fixed-length time fuzes to burst just above the enemy trench and shower the occupants with fragments.

The 2in trench howitzer on its wooden bed ready for use.

With a pair of wheels which appear to be too frail for even the smoothest road, the 2in TH is now ready to travel.

The early mortars soon spread out from the Flanders' trenches. This one is in Mesopotamia. Note the firing mechanism: a cut-down Lee-Enfield rifle action loaded with a blank cartridge, plugged into a vent at the breech and with a lanyard attached to the trigger.

While the British sought simplicity, the Germans, on the other hand, moved in the direction of more complication. They eventually had eight different models of minenwerfer in service, of calibres from 76mm to 250mm, classified as light (76mm), medium (170mm), or heavy (180mm, 240mm and 250mm). By the middle of 1916 there were 281 heavy, 640 medium and 763 light in use, and the production of new ones was proceeding at a rate of 4,300 weapons every month. By the end of the war there were some 17,000 minenwerfers in action, manned by about 200,000 men. The German models became increasingly complicated, with breech-loading, recoil systems, complicated optical sights and luxurious mountings. While the war was static this was of small importance, but in 1918, when things began to move, the liabilities of such heavy weapons soon became apparent.

THE STOKES MORTAR

In Britain a man now appeared whose name was to become permanently attached to the trench mortar. Mr, later Sir, Wilfred Stokes was the managing director of Ransomes and Rapier, a well-known and long-established firm of engineers who had been making agricultural machinery and steam engines for many years. Early in 1915 Stokes began to look at the trench mortar problem, and very soon designed a simple weapon consisting of a smooth-bore barrel with its base resting on a steel baseplate and with the muzzle supported by a bipod with a screw elevating gear. The rear end of the barrel was closed and held a fixed firing pin. The bomb was a simple cylinder of cast iron with a perforated cartridge holder at its rear end holding a 12-bore shotgun cartridge case filled with Ballistite powder. On the front end was a 'pistol', a fuze derived from the striker mechanism of the Mills bomb; a fly-off lever was retained by a safety pin and a spring-loaded plunger. When ready to fire, the pin was removed and the bomb dropped into

the muzzle of the mortar, whereupon it slid down the barrel until the cap of the 12-bore cartridge struck the firing pin. The explosion of the Ballistite lifted the bomb from the barrel, and at the same time the sudden acceleration caused the spring-loaded plunger to 'set back' and free the fly-off lever. This tried to fly off, but could only move a short distance before striking the inside surface of the mortar barrel, and thus could not fly off completely and release its striker until the bomb had left the muzzle. Once clear of the muzzle, the lever flew clear, a striker dropped and fired a cap which began the burning of a nine-second length of safety fuze to give a time-fuze action to the bomb.

Having perfected this device, Stokes offered it to the army. However, by this time there were so many eccentric mortar designs being offered that the army took a long and hard look at any new one before making a commitment. Initially, there were objections to the bomb turning end over end in the air, but Stokes soon showed that in spite of this the weapon was quite accurate. However, to placate the objectors he developed a fin-stabilized bomb which landed on its nose. Then it was claimed that any dirt in the barrel or on the bomb might cause the bomb to stick when loaded. Next came an objection to the fixed firing pin, which, it was averred, threatened to be dangerous if a bomb should misfire; in this case it was necessary to detach the mortar barrel from its baseplate, lift the rear end of the barrel and shake the bomb from the muzzle into the hands of a waiting member of the detachment – a drill which is still followed to this day. Should somebody fumble this move-ment, and the bomb be allowed to slide back onto the fixed firing pin, there was a chance that the second blow might ignite the cartridge, whereupon the mortar would fire, with dire consequences to the man holding it. There was some validity in this argument; indeed, I was once the man holding the barrel of a far more sophisticated mortar than Stokes's when this happened and it can be very alarming to say the least. Stokes countered this with a removable breech-piece which allowed the firing pin to be withdrawn to a safe position before upending the barrel.

Eventually, after several other minor objections had been raised and dealt with, approval was given and the 3in Stokes Mortar entered service in August 1915. While it may seem at first sight that the army was being unnecessarily stubborn about adopting the Stokes design – and one or two politicians made capital out of this delay in later years, claiming that but for their efforts the weapon would never have entered service – the point to be noted is that by raising these objections and getting them corrected the final design was right; it needed very little tinkering with after it entered service and indeed the basic features were repeated in later designs and are perpetuated to this day in descendants of this original pattern. Had it been rushed into service without first ironing out these small but significant points, it would have had a subsequent history of modification and distrust by

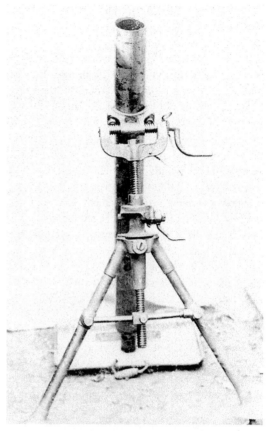

Front view of the original 3in Stokes mortar. Note that there was no sight bracket, nor any means of cross-levelling the barrel to compensate for sloping ground. Direction was given by a stripe of paint on the barrel and elevation by means of a clinometer (a form of adjustable spirit level).

The original Stokes 3in mortar of 1915, in its production form.

the users which would have ruined its effectiveness. As it was, it entered service as a working proposition and was instantly accepted by the troops, being far superior to the models which had gone before.

It might be as well at this point to lay to rest once and for all the oft-repeated story that only political intervention by Lloyd George was responsible for the Stokes being accepted; the Minutes of the Ordnance Board for 1915 carry the full development history of the Stokes, from its initial proposal by Stokes himself to its final

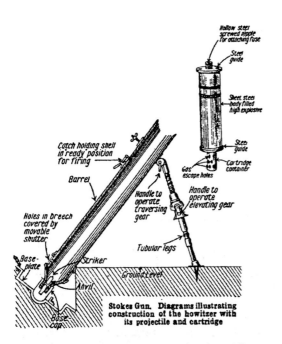

How the Stokes mortar was presented to the public: a contemporary newspaper illustration showing the salient features, some of which (the gas escape holes in the chamber and the catch to hold the bomb ready for firing) never appeared on the Stokes design.

This rare and remarkable picture was discovered in an album of Trench Warfare Department photographs and was labelled 'Anti-Aircraft Version of Stokes 3inch Mortar'. Just how it was proposed to traverse this to keep up with a moving target is something of a mystery; no written details of this conversion have been found.

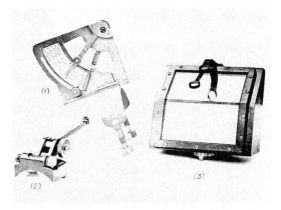

The special sighting apparatus for the anti-aircraft mortar: (1) the elevation scale which clamped to the barrel; (2) the foresight, attached to the muzzle; and (3) a reflecting mirror rear sight which was also clamped to the barrel. Aiming was done by looking through the small eyepiece and aligning the reflection of the foresight with a radial scale of ranges and approach angles which is, unfortunately, too faint to reproduce in this copy.

approval for issue. There is no evidence anywhere in the record of any political influence being brought to bear; it was a simple story of the army and the designer working together to produce a final article with which both were satisfied. Indeed, most of the design work and early trials had been completed well before Lloyd George's Ministry of Munitions was set up.

The primitive 'pistol' fuze was a drawback, since it virtually restricted the weapon to one range, unless the recipients were content to let the bombs lie around until they exploded or the users to settle for short bursts, and it was not long before improvements came along. The first, and easiest, solution was to provide three different fuzes with different times of burning, but this was an unwelcome logistic puzzle and did not last long. Although Stokes had designed a finned bomb, it was considered to be too difficult and

Stokes 4in

Mortar, Stokes, 4in Mark 1

Calibre	4.2in (107mm)
Barrel length	51in (1.295m)
Weight in action	242lb (110kg)
Elevation	+45 degrees to +81.5 degrees
Weight of bomb	25lb (11.3kg)
Muzzle velocity	200 to 450ft/sec (61 to 137m/sec)
Minimum range	200yd (183m)
Maximum range	1,075yd (983m)

The original 4in Stokes mortar. Notice that the small baseplate is bolted to a much larger wooden bed in order to resist digging into the soft ground.

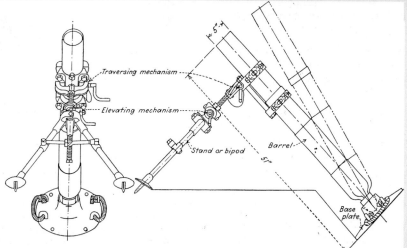

The American version of the 4in Stokes had a circular baseplate but little else was changed. This drawing illustrates the unique feature of the 4in, that the baseplate did not sit flat on the ground but was dug in at an angle.

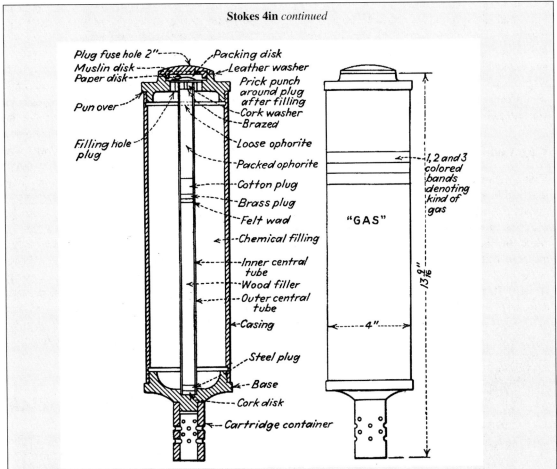

Stokes 4in *continued*

The standard gas bomb for the 4in Stokes; the drawing shows the transport plug in the nose, which would be removed and replaced by a fuze before loading.

The 4in Stokes mortar was specifically designed to fire gas bombs; the 3in Stokes was satisfactory when firing high-explosive bombs, but could not fire a heavy enough bomb to deliver a worthwhile payload of gas. The 6in had a large and capacious bomb, but the rate of fire was too slow to allow a lethal gas cloud to be built up quickly in the target area. The 4in compromised between the two, firing a bomb with three times the capacity of the 3in, having almost equal mobility, and with a burst-fire rate of 20 rounds per minute in order to produce the desired fast build-up of gas or smoke.

The mortar itself was exactly like the 3in, a smooth-bore drawn-steel tube carried on a rectangular baseplate with a simple bipod providing elevation and a limited degree of traverse. The bomb had no pretensions towards aerodynamic shaping, being a simple cylinder with a perforated cartridge container at one end and a 2in fuze hole at the other. But since there was no stabilizing device, the bomb tumbled in flight and consequently the fuze had to be an 'all-ways' fuze which would function at whatever attitude the bomb landed.

The 4in Stokes was discarded by the British Army in the 1920s, the Livens Projector being preferred as a means of delivering gas. But the Americans retained it until it was replaced by the rifled 4.2in M1 mortar in the late 1930s.

expensive a manufacturing proposition at the time, and his original cylindrical bomb was to remain in service throughout the war. In view of its erratic flight through the air there could be no guarantee that it would land nose first, and an 'all-ways' fuze was developed, with a mechanism that would cause the bomb to detonate no matter in what attitude it struck the ground.

Bigger and Better

Stokes followed up his 3in model with a 4in on identical lines, and this, using a larger bomb with greater internal capacity, was largely employed as a means of sending gas into the German lines, while the 3in became primarily a high-explosive weapon. But heavier mortars were still wanted, and soon there came an army-designed 6in heavy mortar. This was somewhat unusual in that it dispensed with the normal form of bipod; the

The 6in Newton mortar with its adjustable bracing wires; getting the correct elevation and traverse must have been a highly skilled business.

barrel rested in a baseplate and was held in the firing position by three support lines of steel wire, adjusted by means of turnbuckles to shorten or lengthen them and thus elevate or depress or traverse the barrel. These were later replaced by rather more robust supports of steel rod which were adjusted by wheel-operated turnbuckles, but the principle remained the same and the 6in actually remained in service as a reserve weapon until some time during the Second World War. The projectile was a 48lb finned bomb carrying a percussion fuze of frightening simplicity in its nose; this was the 'Newton' fuze, produced by a Lt Newton, which relied upon a system he had originally devised for use in a rifle grenade. The fuse was simply a conical steel holder which screwed into the front end of the cylindrical bomb, and had a central hole into which a .303 blank rifle cartridge was inserted. Above it was a spring steel cap carrying a firing pin. When the bomb hit the ground the pin hit the cap of the blank cartridge, which flashed into a detonator and this in turn set off the main filling of the bomb.

THE QUARTER-TO-TEN MORTAR

The heaviest trench mortar used by the British Army was a French 240mm (9.45in) model which was really a muzzle-loading howitzer. At this sort of calibre the mortar ceases to be a simple weapon which can be carried into action by a couple of men and controlled by a corporal with a pair of field glasses and a wet finger, firing bombs out to as far as the eye can conveniently see. It becomes an artillery piece and requires emplacement, a large detachment of men, and some sort of organized fire control and observation. Nevertheless, the large bomb was a useful addition to the trench artillery, although once movement began the 9.45in was usually left behind, and it did not survive the war by many years.

It is, however, notable for producing at least one Victoria Cross. Sgt William Gosling was in

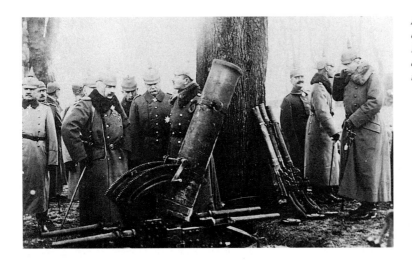

A group of German General Staff officers inspecting a captured British 9.45in mortar, which was actually the French 240mm CT model.

The barrel of the 9.45in mortar in its special transport trolley.

charge of one of these weapons on 5 April 1917 when, due to a faulty propelling charge, the bomb left the barrel and fell only 10yd from the mortar. Gosling well appreciated that the time fuze had

started to burn and within a matter of seconds would detonate the bomb. He jumped from the mortar emplacement, lifted the nose of the bomb from the mud, and, under enemy fire, calmly unscrewed the fuze and threw it aside, whereupon it immediately exploded harmlessly. As the official citation put it, 'This very gallant and unhesitating action undoubtedly saved the lives of the whole detachment.'

THE LIVENS PROJECTOR

The only other British mortar to survive the war without owing anything to Mr Stokes was the little-known 'Livens Projector', a highly specialized mortar designed for one job only – dumping huge quantities of gas into the enemy lines as fast as possible.

The Livens Projector was the invention of a Lt W. H. Livens who was involved in the organizing and operation of the British cloud gas attack at Loos in September 1915. A 'cloud gas attack' was the first method used by both sides, because it was the simplest. The attackers carried hundreds or thousands of cylinders of gas into their front line and, at the appropriate moment, opened the taps. The wind then drifted a cloud of gas across the enemy lines, after which the assault

The Livens Projector

Projector, Livens, ML, 8in Barrel Mks 1–6

Calibre	8.0in (203mm)
Barrel length	33 or 48.1in (838 or 1,222mm)
Weight in action	100lb or 150lb (45.4 or 68kg)
Elevation	45 degrees fixed
Weight of bomb	60lb (27.2kg)
Muzzle velocity	360ft/s (110m/s)
Minimum range	475yd (434m)
Maximum range	1,800yd (1,645m)

The Livens Projector was developed in three barrel lengths, 33, 36 and 48in, though only the 33 and 48in models went into service. The short version gave a maximum range of 1,275yd (1,166m) and the longer one of 1,800yd (1,646m). The device consisted of an 8in (203mm) calibre smooth-bore tube attached to a concave steel baseplate about 20in (508mm) long and 12in (305mm) wide. A trench was dug, the edge towards the enemy being cut at a 45 degrees slope, and the mortars laid in it, pointing towards the enemy, and the earth then shovelled back over them. They were then loaded with a propelling charge of smokeless powder in a circular tin box about 4in (100mm) deep and just under 8in (200mm) in diameter. This contained a number of bags of powder and an electric detonator; the bags permitted various combinations allowing nine different strengths of charge so that some degree of range alteration within the fixed elevation was possible. Electric leads attached to the detonator were led up inside the tube and hung out of the muzzle.

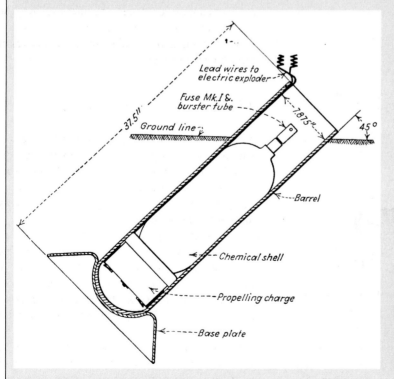

The Livens Projector; simplicity itself. No bipod, the baseplate is welded to the barrel, and the propelling charge is fired by two wires running down above the bomb.

The Livens Projector *continued*

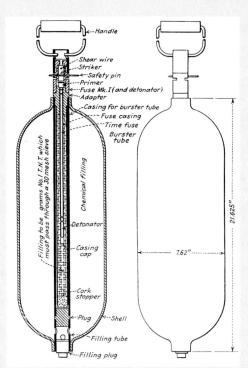

Detail of the Livens bomb or cylinder, showing the central tube which held the 30–36-second fuze and a small burster charge. The handle was removed before loading.

The projectile was a round-ended cylinder of steel with a central tube loaded with high explosive and fitted with a primitive time-fuze. It contained about 30lb (13kg) of liquid gas. The fuze was simply a needle over a cap attached to a length of Bickford safety fuze ending in a detonator, all embedded in the central high-explosive filling and kept safe by means of a safety pin between the firing pin and the cap.

The mortars were emplaced in batteries of twenty-five and then loaded, first with the cartridge and then with the cylinder. The wires dangling from the muzzle were then connected up to a central wire which, in turn, was connected to a firing magneto. When the time for firing approached the safety pins were removed from the fuzes and the entire battery fired as a salvo.

The only real complaint about the Livens Projector was the enormous flash when several hundred were fired at once; the time of flight of the bomb was approximately thirty-five seconds and once the enemy had become familiar with the Livens' flash, that gave enough time for gas sentries to sound the alarm and for everyone get their masks on before the cylinders landed.

The Livens was kept in service in both Britain and the USA during the 1930s, and in 1939 there was considerable effort put into the manufacture of new projectors and cylinders, and preparations for the production of the requisite gas. But nothing further was done and by 1945 the Livens was obsolete.

Loading Livens Projectors. Note that every man has his gas mask at the 'ready' position, with the flap undone, so that if an accident occurs he can mask himself instantly.

took place while the enemy was still coughing and choking. That was the theory, anyway. At Loos the wind suddenly changed just after the taps had been opened, with the result that the gas rolled back over the British attackers.

Livens reasoned that the better solution would be to get the gas cylinder among the enemy before opening it to release the gas. Before he could do anything with his ideas he was put in charge of a flame-thrower company during the Battle of the Somme in 1916, and while so engaged he developed a primitive device for throwing water cans full of flame thrower fluid onto the enemy positions by using an oil drum as a form of mortar. From this humble beginning he began to consider the possibility of fitting some sort of burster to the standard gas cylinder and launching it from a mortar. But the standard gas cylinder weighed about 100lb (45kg), and so launching such a weight from a simple device was not a simple proposition after all.

Eventually his ideas crystallized into the 'Livens Projector', a simple muzzle-loading mortar of 8in calibre. Batteries of these were dug into the ground behind the trenches and loaded with an electrically fired guncotton cartridge and a bomb which was nothing more than a short gas cylinder with a burster charge and time fuze. These bombs held about 30lb (14kg) of gas; once installed and loaded the propelling charges were wired up in series and the whole battery was fired at once.

The first Livens Projectors were fired at Beaumont Hamel in October 1916, more or less as a trial; their effect was satisfactory, even though the weapon was in primitive form and needed perfecting, and arrangements were put in hand for mass production of projectors and bombs. This initial outing appears not to have been appreciated by the Germans, and it also seems to have escaped the notice of the historians; the 'official' date for the first use of Livens Projectors is usually given as 4 April 1917, but Brig-Gen Hartley, who was Assistant Director of Gas Services at GHQ, referred to the Beaumont Hamel operation in a lecture he gave in 1919.

Having proved on a small scale that the weapon was workable, the decision was taken to hold it back until sufficient projectors and bombs were available to bring it into the field in worthwhile numbers, and then not to use it until it could be decisively employed during a major operation. Once unveiled, it could then be used as a weapon of attrition, but it would have been foolish to throw away its surprise value by employing it on day-to-day work. The lesson learned at the Somme, where the tank was thrown in on the wrong ground and in too small numbers, was fresh in many minds, and the Livens Projector promised to be too good a weapon to be squandered in similar fashion.

On Easter Monday, 9 April 1917, the British Army and the Canadian Army attacked at Arras, to take Vimy Ridge and punch a hole in the Hindenburg Line in an assault which was, in its initial stages, one of the most successful battles of the war. As was, however, usual in those days, the reserves and cavalry who were to have poured through the broken German defences failed to materialize and the exhausted infantry could do no more than halt and form a new line. Gen Allenby, the commander of the operation, while a taciturn man who found it difficult to communicate his ideas to others, was nevertheless a very able general and one who was particularly alert to the chance of surprising his enemy with something new. He was also alert to the capabilities of gas when well used, and for the attack at Arras he decided to use not only artillery, but the new Livens Projector as well. Vast amounts of artillery shells filled with chloropicrin, a powerful lung irritant known in British service as 'PS' (because it had been developed in the Lever Brothers' laboratory at Port Sunlight, Cheshire), were now available, together with quantities of Livens bombs filled with 'CG', the British code for phosgene (derived from the French factory at Collonge, where the first Allied supplies were made).

Getting the Livens Projector into action was a simple but laborious task; it was not like a mortar, poised on a baseplate and bipod. The design was far too basic for that, since all the projector consisted of was its wide barrel with a reinforcing plate welded to the bottom: no bipod, no sights, no adjustments of any kind, just a tube. It was emplaced by digging it into the ground; a long trench of V-section, 4ft deep and with the sides angles at 45 degrees, was excavated; the projector barrels were then laid with their bases in the bottom of the trench and their muzzles pointing towards the enemy, just above the surface of the ground. The earth was then shovelled back on top to hold them securely in alignment. One trench would hold anything up to forty projectors, and, naturally, preparation was an activity which was carried out behind the front-line trenches and concealed from the enemy's view.

When the time to fire drew near, the charges of guncotton were placed in the barrels, and their electric firing leads run out from the muzzle. Then the bomb was inserted, the firing wires linked up and tested for continuity, and connected to a firing dynamo. At the last moment the firing officer locked the firing dynamo, took the key in his pocket for his own peace of mind, and then went down the line of projectors pulling out the safety pins from the bomb fuzes. Then he returned to his dynamo, unlocked it once more, lifted the plunger, and at the appointed time rained it down to fire all the projectors at once. A

roar, a blinding flash, and the bombs were hurtling through the air, turning end over end, trailing sparks from their burning fuzes, to land with a thud thirty-five seconds later and a mile away.

At Arras no less than 3,827 projectors threw 51 tons (51,816kg) of phosgene gas into the German trenches in one colossal salvo. A German prisoner afterwards reported that the enormous flash from the projectors was assumed to be an Allied ammunition dump exploding. The incessant drumroll of gunfire common to the Western Front masked the noise of the discharge and flight of the bombs, and the first sign of impending trouble was when the German front line was suddenly enveloped in a thick cloud of phosgene. The concentration was so great that one deep breath was sufficient to kill; before the surprised German troops could put on their gas masks, one hundred men died instantly and a further 500 were later hospitalized, though the full effects of this bombardment were never known.

The most astonishing thing about the Livens Projector is the large numbers in which they were used and the huge quantities of gas which they threw. A thousand projectors were commonplace, and the record appears to have been at St Quentin in March 1918 (prior to the Second Battle of the Somme) when the British employed 5,649 projectors to launch 85 tons (86,560kg) of phosgene, causing 250 deaths and 1,100 men hospitalized.

A row of Livens Projectors ready to be loaded. Note that elevation and direction were not matters to be fussed over; so long as the thing was pointed in the right direction and at about 45 degrees, that was fair enough. The spread of the gas would compensate for any minor discrepancies of aim, and with the odd stray shot you might catch somebody unawares.

Faced with this sort of attack, it is hardly surprising that the Germans set about developing a projector of their own. By late 1917 a number of pioneer battalions had been equipped with an interim design of projector which fired an obsolete 18cm (7in) mortar shall. This was forced on them by the shortage of steel which prevented mass production of a more efficient form of projectile on the lines of the British Livens drum, and the gas content of the bomb was only about half that of the British projectile. In spite of this they used them to good effect, notably in the Battle of Caporetto on the Italian Front in October 1917, when they helped to inflict one of the worst defeats of the entire war.

The Germans then sat down to produce a better projector than the Livens, and in the summer of 1918 began issuing a rifled model, firing a high-capacity shell and capable of reaching to 3,000yd (2,740m) range. Great things were hoped for from this weapon, but in the event relatively few were made and there was little opportunity to use them before the war ended.

Apart from the physical problems entailed in emplacing it, the Livens Projector had one tactical drawback; it was the only missile-throwing weapon solely designed for use with gas munitions and was absolutely useless for anything else. When it wasn't being used to throw gas it wasn't being used at all, and such a lack of flexibility has its drawbacks. Either you have a lot of expensively-trained specialist troops and their equipment sitting doing nothing when not engaged in shooting gas, or you send them off without their equipment to do something useful like mending roads or whitewashing coal piles, and then have the devil's own job to get them back and re-organized for the next gas task. For this reason the trench mortar was a more highly regarded gas weapon on the Allied side; when not firing gas it could be laying smoke screens or firing high explosive shells for the infantry, which kept the mortar troops trained, occupied, and doing something useful all the time. Nevertheless, in 1939 there was a good deal of energy and manufacturing effort put into the manufacture of new Livens Projectors, and measures were also put in train for the necessary supply of gas, should the need arise. Fortunately, it didn't arise, and by 1945 the Livens was practically forgotten and declared obsolete.

FRENCH MORTARS

The French effort in the trench mortar field began in a rather peculiar fashion. The first weapons to be issued were the old 6in Crimean veterans mentioned above, and these were regarded as mere momentary aberrations by the higher command, who took little in the way of steps to provide a better weapon. But the front-line troops felt there was a germ of an idea there. At the same time, another new feature had appeared on the battlefield – barbed wire. The destruction of this was a necessary preliminary to any attack, and it was the job of combat engineers to crawl forward and plant charges to blow up sections of the wire and thus provide gaps for the attacking infantry. Seeing little life expectancy in this activity, a Belgian engineer developed his own system of placing explosive charges in the required spot by throwing them there, using a small explosive propelling charge to launch a stick carrying the blasting charge. As a launcher he used a discarded 75mm gun cartridge case. Having a surplus of cases he decided to experiment with using a few more as offensive projectiles. He placed a wooden mandrel of the correct diameter in the ground and then loaded a charge of explosive and a short length of fuze into a cartridge case. Placing a gunpowder charge on top of the wooden post, along with an electric igniter, the upended cartridge case was now slipped over the post to form a primitive spigot mortar. When the electric igniter was fired the gunpowder blew the explosive-filled case from its mandrel and into the air, to land in the enemy lines with a satisfactory bang.

The projectile was later improved by welding

on three brass fins, cut from another cartridge case, and the design was so successful that it was officially adopted by the French, in a somewhat more elegant design, as the 'Mortier Van Deuren', commemorating the inventor. This was a simple machine, the principal part being a casting which formed a flat baseplate with a stubby barrel fixed at a 45 degree elevation. On to this screwed a narrow, hollow muzzle, alongside which was a bracket carrying electrical terminals. The bomb was the usual teardrop shape, with fins, and with a hollow tail unit. A propelling charge with a short 'tail stick' was inserted into the stub barrel of the mortar so that the actual charge sat on the muzzle; its electric firing leads were laid alongside the stub barrel. The bomb was then loaded by sliding the hollow tail over the

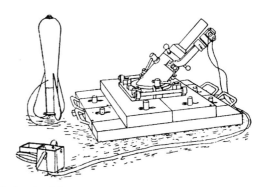

A sketch of the Van Deuren mortar showing the firing magneto and wires and the bomb.

propelling charge and stub barrel, leaving the ends of the propelling charge wires free. These were then led to the terminals on the bracket. The second set of terminals was attached to wires leading a discreet distance to an exploder dynamo – the handle-and-ratchet box containing a magneto, so familiar from cowboy dramas on the films. The box being placed in a safe position, the handle was pushed down, the propelling charge exploded and the bomb was blown off the stub barrel to a range of about 600m (650yd) with a bomb weighing 19kg (42lb). A degree of range adjustment was possible; there were three different strengths of propelling charge, and a screwed collar on the stub barrel could be moved up and down so as to vary the distance which the spigot barrel reached into the bomb and thus vary the size of the explosion chamber. At maximum charge, moving the collar 1cm up the stub barrel would alter the range by about 55m (60yd), so there was a very fine degree of control available.

ENTRY OF THE PROFESSIONALS

The Schneider company was the premier heavy gunmaker of France in those days, and it is hardly surprising that the company was asked to offer suggestions. Its first model was the 'Mortier Tranchée de 75mm Mle 1915' and was simply a small, light breech-loading gun capable of high

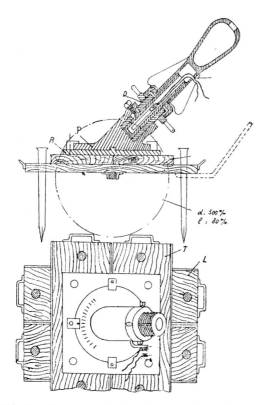

The Van Deuren mortar in section, showing the bomb fitting over the stub barrel, and the propelling charge and its wires in the barrel.

The Schneider 75mm Model of 1915, showing the act of loading.

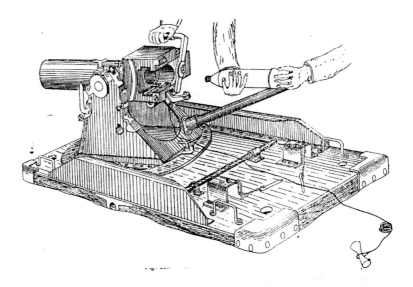

REMOVING A TRENCH GRENADE GUN TO POSITION

A wartime postcard showing the 75mm Schneider mortar being 'moved into position' by a suspiciously clean and tidy detachment.

French 15cm Mortar

Mortier de 150 Tranchée Mle 1916

Calibre	150mm (5.9in)
Barrel length	1,750mm (69in)
Weight in action	600kg (1,323lb)
Elevation	+45 degrees to +76.5 degrees
Weight of bomb	18kg (39.6 lb)
Muzzle velocity	145m/sec (476ft/sec)
Minimum range	500m (547yd)
Maximum range	1,900m (2,080yd)

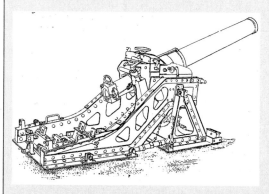

The 15cm Mle 1916 mortar in the firing position; the mounting is in two sections, the forward support and the trail, hinged together and linked by turnbuckles.

This mortar was rather unusual insofar as it was loaded from *both* ends, muzzle and breech. There were two reasons for this. Firstly, speed: while the bomb was going in at one end the cartridge was going in at the other. Secondly, ballistic efficiency: in the late eighteenth century it was discovered that a 'chambered' mortar – that is, a large-calibre mortar with a much smaller calibre of chamber formed in the base end of the bore – used powder more efficiently, because the explosion took place in a more confined space and thus built up pressure faster. The gas thus generated then passed into the main body of the mortar where it could expand and perform its propellant function. This 15cm weapon had a 15cm barrel, but the lower section was fitted with a reduced-diameter chamber insert in which the cartridge was exploded.

The breech closure was, to say the least, primitive; simply a sliding metal plate that dropped into a slot in the breech end of the barrel. It was pierced with a hole, central to the chamber, into which went a firing pin, and there was a large hammer hinged on the side of the breech ring which could be driven onto the pin by pulling a lanyard.

The bomb was a modern-looking projectile with six fins, weighing 18kg and containing 5.4kg of explosive. It was fitted with one of five different types of percussion fuze at various stages in its service; one problem was

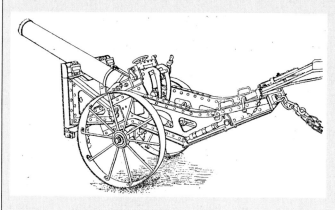

The Mle 1916 ready for the road; the forward support has been hinged forward beneath the barrel and an axle with wheels attached to the trail unit.

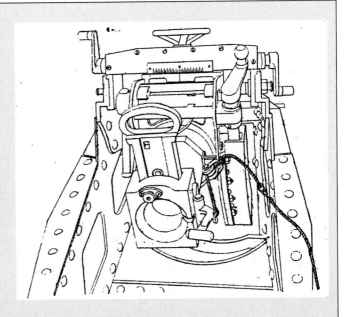

The breech end of the Mle 1916, showing the simple construction.

finding a fuze sensitive enough to detonate the bomb as it plunged into the ever-present mud, but not so sensitive as to go off prematurely at the shock of discharge. The cartridge was made up from two bags of Ballistite powder packed into a cut-down 75mm gun cartridge case.

The barrel was carried in two side-plates built up from girder iron; it could be traversed a small amount by two handwheels above the breech, though larger movements involved lifting the mounting off the ground and realigning it. It could be fitted with wheels for horse-drawn movement or pushed by its detachment for short distances.

elevations. It sat on a simple mounting attached to a wooden baseplate, and the mortar barrel had a very simple (and not very strong) sliding block breech mechanism. Brackets on the baseplate allowed for the attachment of two wheels and two handles to allow it to be pushed like a wheelbarrow. There was very little to go wrong with it; the shell and cartridge were conventional artillery pattern although the cartridge case was very short, and it fired a 5kg (11lb) shell (originally designed for a mountain howitzer) to a range of 1,700m (1,860yd).

The army found this weapon acceptable, and, as might be expected, asked Schneider to produce something more powerful. Schneider obliged with the 'Mortier Tranchée 15cm Mle 1916',

another simple breech-loader. This was trunnioned into a heavy iron frame, with the usual facility for attaching wheels and handles for moving it about, and the breech was even more primitive than the 75mm model. In some respects it resembled the first Armstrong breech-loading guns of 1864; the barrel ended in a square-section breech ring, with a hole in the middle to allow access to the chamber. At the rear end of the chamber, and some centimetres forward of the rear end of the breech ring, there was a vertical slot into which a steel plate with a handle was dropped and held by a spring catch. That was the breechblock, and it had a hole in the centre for a firing pin. To load, the mortar was brought to the horizontal and the bomb loaded into the muzzle;

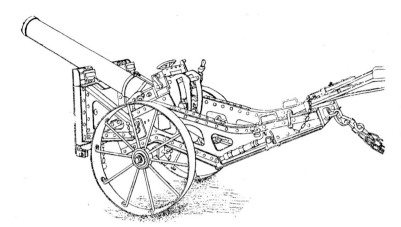

The 15cm Schneider Model 1916. The design shows the reluctance to forget the traditional gun and carriage assembly. In this case there was a platform which folded up under the barrel and could be dropped down, the wheels removed, and finally the trail laid down at the rear.

at the same time, the plate was lifted out and the propelling charge, inside a cut-down cartridge case, was inserted into the rear end. The plate was dropped back into the breech, to be retained by a catch, the mortar elevated and then fired by a lanyard which drove a hammer onto the firing pin. As the Frenchman said of of the early automobile gearbox, '*C'est brutal, mais ça marche!*', and it launched an 18kg (40lb) bomb to 1,900m (2,080yd).

Next in line came a 15cm mortar, known as the 'Matériel Mle 1917' or 'Mortier Fabry', from its designer. It was very similar in general appearance – a girder structure supporting a short-barrelled breech-loader – but had some luxurious appendages. It had, for example, the mortar mounted upon a top carriage, allowing a considerable amount of traverse without having to move the baseplate; and it had two recoil and recuperator cylinders alongside the barrel to soak up some of the firing energy. It fired a 17kg (38lb) finned bomb to a range of 2,000m (2,190yd).

In spite of the fact that the Mle 1917 weighed 600kg (1,323lb) in action, all the foregoing French mortars were officially classified as matériels légère – light equipments. The heavy brigade consisted of two models, of 24cm and 31cm calibre. The '24cm Mortier Lourde Tranchée' was another Schneider design and was,

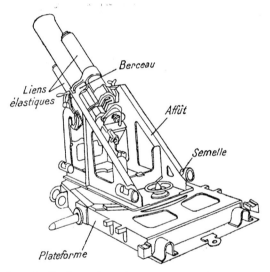

It gradually dawned on the designers that trench mortars were not called upon to move very often, and that therefore complex carriage arrangements were a waste of effort. The 15cm Schneider Model 1917 reflects this, with a simple platform and top carriage, the former having stub axles for attaching wheels.

so far as the mortar itself went, simply an enlarged version of the 15cm, with the same primitive breech closure. In this case, though, the ignition of the charge was a trifle more sophisticated – a self-cocking firing mechanism was provided as a separate unit into which a blank rifle cartridge was clipped and then the whole

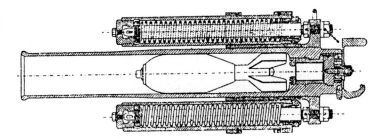

The Schneider Model 1917 also boasted a rather elegant recoil system in which two cylinders were used, each combining the functions of oil buffer and spring recuperator.

affair was plugged into a hole in the breech closing plate and given half a turn to secure it. A lanyard was hooked onto the trip mechanism and a quick jerk cocked and released the firing pin to fire the blank cartridge and thus the main charge behind the bomb. The mounting consisted of two toothed segments bolted down into a cast-iron base mounted on a substantial timber bed. By winding a handle the barrel was propelled around the toothed segment to give whatever elevation was desired from zero to 90 degrees, though it was only fired between 45 degrees and 75 degrees, the extreme positions being only for travelling or loading. The mortar fired an 81kg (179lb) finned bomb to a maximum range of 1,365m (2,150yd). The all-up weight was 882kg (1,945lb) plus another 2,600kg (5,733lb) for the wooden platform – about 3½ tons. There was also a shorter version – the Mortier de 240 C.T. – which fired the same bomb to about 1,000m (1,094yd). This version was the one which went into British service as the 9.45in Trench Mortar.

The 31cm 'Mortier de 310 Tranchée' was a substantial piece of equipment which had to be carefully emplaced and was not, by any means, in the 'shoot-and-scoot' category. The whole thing weighed 3,195kg (7,045lb) and required an emplacement to be excavated and a semicircle of railway line laid at the front of this, so that a small trolley with a loading platform could be pushed around to line up with the barrel for loading. This trolley carried a sloping tray on which the bomb, weighing 195kg (430lb) and loaded with 93kg (205lb) of high explosive, was lifted by a small

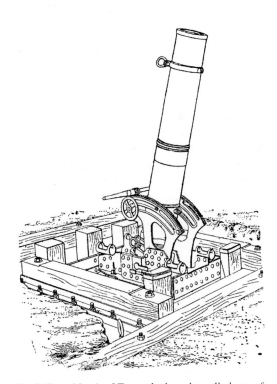

The 240mm Mortier LT was the long-barrelled one of a pair, the short one being the CT and used also by the British. This drawing shows the elevating system in which the two toothed arcs were fixed and the crank handle rotated cogwheels to move the barrel across the arcs. Once at the correct elevation, the handwheel was turned to lock the barrel in place.

crane. The barrel, which was on a similar mounting to the 240mm model, a pair of toothed segments around which the tube could be elevated, was brought down to the loading angle of about 25 degrees, the trolley pushed around to

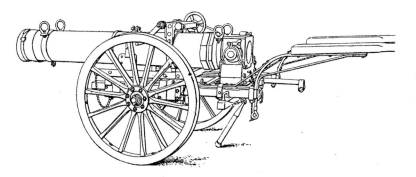

Instead of the usual method of attaching wheels to the mortar bed, the 240mm was so large that the barrel travelled separately on its own cart. Wheels were then attached to the bed for its movement.

The 310mm mortar was simply an enlarged version of the 240mm LT. This drawing shows the emplaced mortar and the stretch of Decauville trench railway track laid in front to carry the loading wagon.

line up with it and the bomb loaded by pushing into the muzzle. At the same time, the breech cap was removed and the charge introduced into a reduced-diameter chamber at the rear end of the barrel. Having rammed the bomb down as far as it would go, the tube was then elevated and fired by a percussion lock inserted into the rear of the breech cap. The bomb had a maximum range of 2,300m (2,515yd) and could produce a quite impressive crater when it landed.

AMERICA'S MORTARS

When the US Army entered the war it found itself confronted with an entirely new weapon, having never contemplated trench mortars before. After reviewing the various patterns in use by the various armies, the US Army selected the British 3in, 4in and 6in and the French 24cm CT models

as being best suited to its use, and set about manufacturing them in the USA. Contracts for about 4,500 3in, 500 4in, 1,677 6in and 938 24cm mortars were issued from late 1917 to the spring of 1918 but, as with much of the American munitions programme, very little appeared before the war had ended.

The Americans were also very much impressed by the Livens Projector, seeing it as the ideal method of delivering gas, and set up a major production programme. By the end of the war over 63,000 barrels and 100,000 baseplates had been produced, together with a vast array of accessories, and contracts for the production of 334,000 cylinders were well under way. An entire new arsenal at Edgewood, Maryland, was devoted to the production of toxic gas and the filling of it into mortar bombs and Livens Projector cylinders. But the end of the war saw the contracts severely reduced and although the

Livens Projector was still highly thought of in the middle 1930s, it was never revived during World War II.

UNORTHODOX PROPELLANTS

So far, we have been considering mortars which propelled their bombs by the explosion of some form of propelling powder, either gunpowder or smokeless powder. But there were other methods in use during the First World War which are worth a mention. The great problem in the early days was producing a smokeless weapon, since with the early gunpowder charges the cloud of white smoke produced when the mortar was fired meant certain retaliation by the offended enemy. The production of smokeless powder, certainly during the first half of the war, was barely sufficient to keep up with the demands of artillery and small arms, and very little could be spared for trench mortars; hence the use of gunpowder or, in some cases, guncotton, which is a notably unreliable propelling charge. In addition to the smoke problem, it would have been advantageous to have a silent means of propulsion, so as to be able to drop bombs into enemy trenches at night without heralding their approach by the discharge of the mortar; since mortars had a high trajectory, the bomb also had a long flight time, meaning that if the enemy heard the mortar fire they had ample time in which to take cover.

The first British solution to this problem could hardly be termed a mortar, but it deserves a mention as being one of the less-explored byways of ordnance: the West Spring Gun. Designed by an officer named West, this was in fact no more than the mediaeval catapult brought up to date and propelled by massive coil springs as opposed to the twisted rawhide and ropes of old. The arm of the machine ended in a cup of the right size to hold a hand grenade No. 5 (the original Mills Bomb). It was brought down to the horizontal, against the power of the springs, by various leverage devices, and then locked. A hand grenade was placed in the cup, the pin withdrawn and the arm immediately released. According to how much tension had been set on the springs, the range was anything from 70 to 150yd and, of course, it was both smokeless and (more or less) silent. But it hardly advanced the science of ballistics.

Two serious solutions then come under consideration: compressed air or inflammable gas. Although several designs of this sort were offered to the Allies, only a handful of pneumatic mortars were adopted by the French Army. However, the Germans were never averse to trying new ideas, and the German Army produced a few specimens operated by acetylene gas. A metered amount of acetylene was introduced into the chamber of the mortar after the bomb had been loaded, to combine with the air already present to form an explosive mixture. It was then ignited by a percussion cap so as to explode and propel the bomb from the barrel. Theoretically, the efficiency of the gas–air mixture ought to have been on a par with the more common propellant explosives, but in practice this did not

Captain West's Spring Gun, a highly complex and expensive method of flinging a hand grenade, but one which gave it a startling range and a completely silent method of delivery.

happen. The metering of the acetylene gas was generally insufficiently precise to form the most effective gas–air mixture, and the mixing of the gas and air in the chamber was not as thorough as it would have been in laboratory conditions. Hence the range of this class of mortar was somewhat less than the predicted figure and not up to the standard of conventionally propelled weapons. In spite of this, and in spite of the problems of maintaining a supply of gas in the field, these weapons served throughout the war, generally in the less-involved sectors of the Front. While they still made a noise when fired, it was described as being 'softer' than the sound of normal explosives, and according to some reporters was usually lost in the general drum roll of gunfire which formed a constant background, so that some degree of surprise was attained. Their only other virtue was that they economized on conventional propelling powders, a fact which made them of greater value as the war went on.

The Austro-Hungarian Army adopted five compressed-air models, of 80mm, 105mm, 120mm, 170mm and 200mm calibres. The largest of these had a range of 1,800m (1,970yd), which was certainly an impressive performance from such a weapon and it appears, from contemporary documents, that the principal reason for adopting them was, again, the shortage of smokeless propellant powder. This meant that the standard types of mortar were all using black powder, with its attendant smoke problem. Thus the official

regulations decreed that the powder-firing weapons would be used for night firing only, while the pneumatic mortars could be used by day or night.

The pneumatic principle of operation had been explored years before by both the US Army and British Army when they tested the 'Zalinski Pneumatic Dynamite Cannon' in the 1880s and 1890s, and during the war years it was again revived on the Allied side in the Sims-Dudley Pneumatic Field Gun, but there was no enthusiasm for such weapons and the Allies never employed them.

The Austrian mortars used cylinders of compressed air connected to the rear of the barrel; the bomb was lowered into the mortar and then a quick-acting valve was opened to deliver a burst of high-pressure air to the chamber to blow the bomb from the barrel. While the system was effective, it could only be maintained in a static position due to the problem of supplying and recharging the air cylinders, and doubtless the infantrymen of the Austro-Hungarian Army had a few words to say on the subject as they slogged through the mud and darkness with large cylinders of compressed air on their backs to resupply the forward positions. It appears, in fact, that in the latter part of the war the light model was dropped from the inventory and the heavy calibres were assigned to artillery, a sixth battery being added to the field artillery regiment, armed entirely with pneumatic mortars. This probably simplified the air supply problem.

4 Edgar Brandt and Others

When World War I ended most of the minenwerfers and trench mortars were scrapped out of hand; it has to be admitted that most of them were designs which no self-respecting army would wish to be seen with in peacetime. Moreover, there was a feeling that most of these contraptions were aberrations due entirely to the conditions which had held sway from 1915 to mid-1918 and that they were unlikely ever to be needed again. A few of the better models were kept in reserve, but these were no longer considered as first-line weapons, and the training schedules of the early 1920s rarely considered the mortar.

But during the latter half of the 1920s a subject of discussion which came to be heard more and more among the world's armies was the matter of close support for infantry. The French had initiated matters with their introduction during the war of a 37mm trench cannon, a useful little weapon that provided the front-line soldiers with some personal artillery, and the Germans had also given their infantrymen a number of light 75mm guns and howitzers, most of which had originally entered service as mountain or pack artillery weapons. These, together with the mortars supplied in such profusion, had allowed the infantry to bring immediate heavy firepower to bear on any small nuisance which presented itself, and it was this instant support they were anxious to retain. The arguments waxed loud and long and largely obscured the prime issue, which was simply that so long as the shell fell in the right place, it did not much matter where it came from. If the artillery observers could be given adequate and foolproof communication with their gun

The 37mm M1916 trench cannon was a French equipment adopted (as here) by the US Army in 1918. It was a praiseworthy attempt to give the infantry some mobile heavy firepower, but of limited ability due to its near-flat trajectory.

batteries and a suitably fast system of fire control, then they would be able to give all the support the infantry needed without the latter having to drag their own artillery about with them. The prime function of the artillery was, is and always will be, to shoot the infantry onto their objective and protect them once they are there, and the only thing that prevented them from giving the infantry the instant response they needed was the difficulty of getting orders back to the guns. Since there appeared to be no immediate solution to this dilemma – for radio communication was still in its infancy and depended on the phase of the moon and the flexibility of the cat's whisker, or so it seemed – the infantry had a reasonable case for some sort of heavy weapon.

But giving the infantry a conventional howitzer, no matter how light and handy, would hardly solve the problem. These weapons would cost the same as the standard field artillery weapons, the ammunition would be as complicated and expensive, and they would each need six or seven soldiers to man and shift them, plus some sort of traction, be it horses or motor vehicle, to get them to the scene of the action. The British Army first proposed forming 'Light Batteries' of the Royal Artillery, arming them with 3.7in mountain howitzers. But given the financial restrictions on manpower which prevailed at the time, men who were operating infantry support weapons would not be operating field or medium or heavy artillery, and thus the organizational strength of those formations would be weakened and the divisional artillery strength might have to be reduced. And although there were sufficient 3.7in howitzers left over from the war, the provision of the necessary motor vehicles, drivers and so forth was another financial problem. The more the question was studied, both in Britain and elsewhere, the more attractive the mortar seemed to be, and, one by one, most armies began to look towards a mortar of about 3in/80mm calibre firing a bomb of about 10lb/4kg to something in the order of 2,000yd/1,800m range, as the solution to their problem.

THE BRANDT MORTARS

By this time, there were only two contenders in the field: the Stokes mortar and a similar design developed by the French designer Edgar Brandt. Brandt came into the mortar business by making pneumatic trench mortars for the French Army in

A 1935 advertisement for the Brandt mortars, showing their basic 81mm model.

1917. He then looked at the 3in Stokes and saw one or two points which could be improved and in the 1920s went into business making mortars for export sale. The success of the Brandt 81mm mortar made it the standard infantry mortar throughout the world, and the 81mm Mortar M1927/31 became the classic mortar of its era, so that by 1939 all the first-line armies had (and most of them still have) in service at least one type of 81mm mortar from Brandt's drawing board. The 81mm calibre became a standard international calibre, and the Brandt mortars were sold to, licence-built, or copied by, most of the world's armies.

The 81mm mortar, constantly improved, was soon followed by a 60mm mortar for the company level and then by several other types of mortar, from a 47mm platoon light mortar to various types of 120mm mortar intended for the infantry regiment level, or as light field artillery weapons. By the beginning of 1939 the complete range of Brandt mortars included the following:

- 47mm platoon light mortar, range 900m (985yd)
- 57mm company light mortar; range 1,880m (2,060yd)
- 60mm Model 1934 mortar, range 1,760m (1,925yd); a company weapon, this mortar was adopted by the French Army, and licence-built

in the USA under the nomenclature Mortar, 60mm, M2

- the 81mm mortar M19927/31 with a range of 3,100m (3,390yd) was the battalion (heavy weapons company) equipment; this mortar, already adopted by the French Army, was also licence-built in the USA as the Mortar, 81mm, M1

The US 60mm M2 was a licence-built Brandt design.

Another view of the US 60mm M2, showing its compact dimensions.

- the 81mm light mortar M1939, with a range of 2,000m (2,190yd), was intended for the company level and as a future replacement for the 60mm designs where heavier firepower was wanted.

Two further 81mm designs were offered at battalion level: the 81mm high power light mortar with a range of 5,000m (5,470yd) and the 81mm long-range towed mortar, with a range of 6,200m (6,780yd). In fact, very few of these had been made or sold before 1939, but they were to form the basis of post-war designs. Another, and more important innovation, was a range of 120mm mortars which Brandt developed in the mid-1930s. The 120mm light towed mortar had a range of 3,900m (4,270yd) and was intended as a heavy support weapon for the infantry regiment or battalion. The 120mm field mortar, towed, with a range of 7,000m (7,660yd), was proposed as a field artillery weapon, as was the 120mm T35 heavy towed mortar, which had a slightly better range of 8,000m (8,750yd). Numbers of these mortars were sold to China, Japan and Russia, and

The Brandt 120mm light model, a pioneering venture which failed to gain much of a following before 1940.

some of these saw action in Nomonhan and other Russo-Japanese border engagements in 1939–40, as a result of which the Russians set about developing their own 120mm mortar a move that was to have far-reaching effects.

THE PLATOON MORTAR

The British opted to keep their tried and tested 3in Stokes, improving it somewhat in minor details but keeping the same basic configuration of baseplate, bipod and barrel and developing a better-shaped bomb and a more reliable fuze. Once the infantry had their hands on this, the cry for support artillery quietened, and they began looking for something lighter to supplement rifle-launched grenades. The between-wars' grenade of the British Army was the No. 54, a somewhat unsatisfactory design, and it was thought that a light mortar, or, as some called it, a 'grenade discharger', might be a useful tool for the infantry platoon. Designs were studied during the 1930s, and in about 1934 a Spanish design, the Ecia 50mm mortar, was purchased and tested. The name Ecia was a contraction of the company name, Esperanza y Compania, which had quietly moved into the mortar business in the late 1920s with some designs generally based upon the Brandt model but with a few individual touches.

Another submission was a grenade launcher designed by Lt Col Blacker, a Royal Artillery officer whom we shall meet again. Blacker was a great protagonist of the 'Spigot Mortar', a system in which the mortar's business end was a solid steel rod instead of a hollow tube, and the projectile had a hollow tail which was slipped over the rod to load. The cartridge was inside this tail unit and, on being fired, the explosion blew the bomb off the rod; one of the principal advantages claimed was that the manufacture of barrels was probably the greatest bottleneck in weapon manufacture, and dispensing with the barrel and replacing it with something as simple as a steel rod would improve the supply position in wartime. There was also an advantage in that as long as the interior of the tail tube was the correct dimension, the rest of the bomb did not matter, and bombs of any size or shape could be fired from the same spigot. Nonetheless, the design was turned down, since although the weapon itself appeared to be relatively simple, the design of the bomb was held to be too complicated. Within a month, Blacker returned with a new set of designs which did away with many of the objections and the Parnall Aircraft Company was given a contract to produce one weapon, with some 60–70 bombs, for trial.

A 2.5in calibre mortar developed by the Birmingham Small Arms Company was also on offer, plus one or two others of about the same calibre, and late in 1937 a comparative test was held of all the possible designs. The Spanish Ecia proved to be superior to all the others, and the military design department set about making some modifications to simplify manufacture. Once this had been done ten mortars, together with 1,600 high-explosive and 1,600 smoke bombs, were ordered for troop trials in November 1937. The result of this trial was confirmation that the design was sound, and the Director of Artillery, responsible for weapon procurement,

The Spanish-designed 2in mortar became the British infantry's platoon weapon.

decided in February 1938 to go ahead with an order for 500 2in mortars, together with the necessary ammunition, without waiting for further evaluation or discussion. These were, of course, made under licence in Britain, for by then the Ecia firm was embroiled in the Spanish Civil War.

The full flowering of the 2in mortar was this Mark 7 version, complete with adjustable sight and carrying handle. The wooden base was purely for photographic purposes; the normal baseplate, seen here, had a toothed under-surface which dug into the ground.

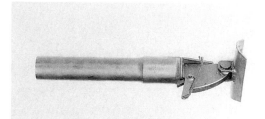

The Mark 8 2in mortar was designed for use by airborne troops and had a minimal baseplate; it proved to be perfectly satisfactory and more or less replaced the Mark 7 after the war.

However good a weapon may be, there is always somebody trying to do better. This was the Weston 2in mortar of 1944 which featured an automatically re-cocked firing mechanism. It proved difficult to use in soft ground and unreliable, and was refused.

UK 3 inch

Ordnance, Smooth-Bore (SB), Muzzle-Loading (ML), 3in Mortar

Calibre	3in (76mm)
Barrel length	51in (1.295m)
Weight in action:	112 lb (50.8kg)
Elevation	45–90 degrees
Traverse	5.5 degrees right or left
Weight of bomb	10lb (4.54kg)
Maximum range	1,600yd (1,463m) (Mk 1); 2,800yd (2,560m) (Mk 2)
Rate of fire	10 rd/min

A British 3in mortar in action in the Libyan desert, 1942.

The 3in mortar was the descendant of the Stokes 3in of World War I, and since the original Stokes had been the ancestor of all post-war mortars the British 3in was much the same as its foreign contemporaries. It fired a fin-stabilized bomb by means of a charge consisting of a primary cartridge in the tail unit and four secondary cartridges, celluloid tubes containing smokeless powder, tucked between the tail fins and retained by a wire spring.

The breech end of the mortar rested on a baseplate, and the muzzle end was supported by a bipod with screw elevating and traversing arrangements. To reduce the effect of firing shock on the mounting, the barrel was free to slide in the yoke of the bipod and was controlled by two tension springs clipped to a barrel band.

As originally developed, the mortar had a maximum range of 1,600yd (1,460m) but, like every weapon since the dawn of time, the users were soon asking for more range. By adopting a slightly heavier barrel of stronger steel and a stronger baseplate, it was found possible to adopt a secondary propelling charge which sent the bomb

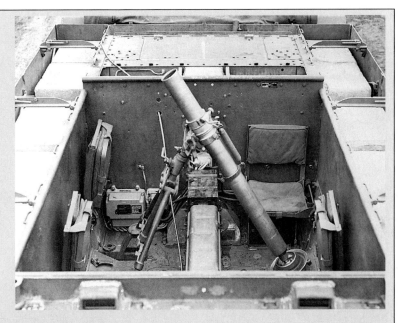

A 3in mortar mounted in an Oxford Carrier, a 1945 experiment in mortar mobility.

to 2,800yd (2,560m), and this Mark 2 model became standard.

Much experimental work was done during the war in an endeavour to obtain even greater range; a barrel in 40-ton steel was developed but with the extra propelling charge necessary to reach the target of 4,000yd (3,650m), even this barrel began to bulge. A fresh design in 50-ton steel was then made, which withstood firings but with an accuracy far below the standard the users were willing to accept. Eventually, in 1945, it was agreed that trying to extract more performance from this design was pointless, and work began on the development of an entirely new mortar, which, after many experimental models in a variety of calibres, led to the present-day 81mm mortar.

Variants

There were several minor variations which were largely concerned with special clips and brackets to suit particular methods of transportation. The Canadian Army developed a model with an 81in (2,060mm) barrel which, it was hoped, would give longer range; but the increase was only 300yd (275m), while the weight had gone up by 32lb (14.9kg), so the design was dropped. The Australians, on the other hand, were more concerned with lightness and portability in the jungle than with extremes of range, and their development was a version with a barrel only 30in (760mm) long. This led to some difficulty in obtaining accuracy, and eventually special fast-burning cartridges had to be produced to suit this short mortar. It was only made in small numbers and was never adopted outside the Australian Army.

THE RIFLED MORTAR

The United States Army Chemical Warfare Service had retained its 4in Stokes mortars after the war ended in 1918 and, having purchased a stock of ammunition from Britain, decided to spend the next few years improving the weapon's range and accuracy.

In 1919, an Australian Army Officer, Capt R. H. S. Abbot, submitted a design of mortar shell to the British Ordnance Board which would allow the barrel of the mortar to be rifled while still permitting the bomb to be drop-loaded from the muzzle. His idea was to fit a soft brass or copper disc at the base of the shell, surrounding the propellant cartridge container; this disc had a flanged edge which was of the same external diameter as the shell body, so that it could be entered into the muzzle of the mortar. Beneath this was a saucer-shaped steel plate.

When the shell was loaded, the explosion of the propelling charge would flatten the steel saucer, so increasing its diameter, and this would force the flanged edge of the copper plate out to bite into the rifling of the barrel and so spin the bomb on its way out, giving the projectile better stability and accuracy, and also, since it trapped the gas behind the shell more effectively, improving the efficiency of the weapon. Abbot had modified some 18-pounder gun shells and fired them from an experimental mortar successfully, but the Ordnance Board turned down the idea: 'Rifling would vitiate the simplicity which is an inherent feature of the Stokes mortar' they claimed, and that was that. The subsequent activities of Capt Abbot are unrecorded, but the fact remains that his design turned up five years later in the USA. A Capt Lewis M. McBride of the Chemical Warfare Service had been given the job of reworking the 4in Stokes design, and in 1924 he produced a 4.2in rifled mortar using a shell with the Abbot system of sealing plate at the bottom.

This promised to be an excellent weapon, with a sizeable bomb, a range of about 2,000yd (1,830m) and a high degree of accuracy, but by the middle of the 1920s the shortage of funds which afflicted every army was making itself felt in the USA and few of these 4.2in mortars were made or issued. Eventually, in 1935, manufacture was stopped completely, and the Chemical Warfare Service (CWS) was ordered to revert to using the 81mm Brandt design. This at least meant that everybody in the US Army was using the same mortar, but bearing in mind that the original purpose of the 4.2in was to dump large quantities of gas into the enemy lines in a short time, its replacement by the 81mm was a backward step as far as the CWS was concerned. The CWS pointed out that eight 4.2in mortars could deliver over a ton of gas in two minutes, but

by 1936 gas had become a naughty word and the CWS was not considered important enough to warrant its own private brand of mortar. However, the CWS was not daunted; indeed, it had foreseen this attitude and had quietly taken a step which was, in the long run, to alter its whole function. As early as 1934 it had looked into the possibility of firing high-explosive ammunition from its mortars as a secondary role, should gas warfare become outlawed, and experiments had shown encouraging results. With this ace up its sleeve the, CWS decided to wait and see what was going to happen next; in the event, it had to wait until the war broke out before it could play its card.

MORE CHEMICAL WARFARE

The British 4.2in mortar also appeared from the chemical warfare stable. During the First World War the mortar and gun as a means of delivering large quantities of gas at short ranges had been largely superseded by the Livens Projector. But the Livens had numerous drawbacks: its range was short, it had to be laboriously dug into the ground, it was slow to reload, it absorbed large numbers of men to operate the serried ranks of mortars usually used, and it had absolutely no other function beyond discharging gas canisters. In the early 1930s the search began for some system that would be more flexible, easier to emplace, use less men, and still deliver a reasonable amount of gas. Reports of the effectiveness of the US 4.2in were studied and work began, on low priority, to produce a smooth-bore 4.2in for British chemical warfare units. The eventual design, produced shortly before the outbreak of war in 1939, was little more than an enlarged version of the 3in, and it was hoped that it would be able to reach out to 4,000yd (3,660m) with a high-explosive bomb and 2,600yd (2,380m) with a chemical bomb. However, the design of the baseplate would not stand the recoil blow of a charge heavy enough to

US 81mm

Mortar, 81mm Ml on mount Ml

Calibre	81mm (3.16in)
Barrel length	49.5in (1.257m)
Weight in action	136lb (61.7kg)
Elevation	40–85 degrees
Traverse	5 degrees right or left
Weight of bomb	HE M43 6.871b (3.12kg); HE M36 10.62lb (4.82kg); smoke M57 10.75lb (4.88kg)
Maximum range	3,290yd (3,008m) (M43); 2,558yd (2,340m) (M36); 2,470yd (2,259m) (smoke)
Rate of fire	18rd/min

The United States Army adopted the Stokes 3in mortar in 1918 and retained numbers of them after the war ended. As the Stokes, in its 1918 guise, was somewhat primitive, work began in 1920 to improve it, with particular emphasis on improving the accuracy of the finned bomb. While this work was in progress the French firm of Edgar Brandt had developed an 81mm mortar based on Stokes's design, and offered this model to the US War Department for test. As it appeared to meet the specifications stated by the Army, a number were purchased for evaluation. Subsequent tests proving successful, the manufacturing rights were purchased from Brandt and the weapon entered US service in the early 1930s.

It was originally provided with two high-explosive bombs, a 'light' and a 'heavy'. The latter had an unusual type of fin assembly consisting of four fins, each with a pair of spring-loaded fins at its outer edge. These spring units were folded up and secured by soft rivets until fired, when the force of the explosion drove a shearing ring forward

The 81mm mortar M1 together with its light and heavy bombs.

67

US 81mm *continued*

Laying a mortar is a two-man job; one uses the sight to align with his aiming mark, while the other man adjusts the cross-level and elevation. Since the mortar is an essentially three-legged beast, adjustment of any one factor affects the other two.

and cut the rivets, allowing the fins to open out under spring pressure once the bomb had left the muzzle. Once unfolded, the fins were of greater calibre than the bomb, thus they were well out into the airstream to give the bomb excellent stability. While theoretically very sound – indeed, Brandt was some years ahead of anyone else in appreciating the value of super-calibre fins – it was found in practice that the springs tended to lose their tension in storage and the cartridge explosion often bent or warped the fins, leading to unstable or inaccurate flight. As a result, this bomb, the M45, was declared obsolete in March 1940 and replaced by the M56 model of the same weight and general appearance but with a cluster of conventional fins.

Variants

There were no variant models of either mortar or mount. However, there were a variety of self-propelled carriages provided or proposed which are summarized here:

- Mortar carrier M4 or M4AI – the 81mm mortar installed in the bed of a half-track weapons carrier, firing to the rear.
- Mortar carrier M21 (T19) – similar to M4 but firing to the front, over the cab.
- Mortar carrier T27 – this project was believed to involve a tank chassis; initiated in April 1944, it was closed down shortly afterwards.
- Mortar carrier T27EI – a spin-off from the T27, this was intended to use redundant light tank chassis without turrets; begun in April 1944, it was closed down about a year later without having shown any result.

---

send the cylindrical high-explosive bomb to the desired range, only 3,300yd (3,020m) being possible. The design was changed for a stream-lined bomb that, although reducing the weight of high explosive carried, allowed the desired range to be reached with a worthwhile payload. This mortar was officially approved for issue in March 1942, although numbers actually began entering service late in 1941.

During the development phase various other designs had been put forward; a 5in mortar with a maximum range of 2,000yd (1,830m) was

demanded in October 1939, but the progress of the war showed that this, while it would have been suitable for trench warfare as envisaged in October 1939, was insufficient for a war of movement, and the requirement was cancelled in early 1942. It was recast and revived again in April 1943, this time as a super-heavy mortar to range to 6,000yd (5,490m). Work went on slowly throughout the war, perfecting bomb designs, but this proved to be difficult and in August 1945 it too was dropped.

The development of the 4.2in had been attended by a number of 'teething troubles', and

UK 4.2in

Ordnance, ML, SB, 4.2in Mortar Mark 1

Calibre	4.2in (107mm)
Barrel length	68.1in (1.73m)
Weight in action:	271lbs (123kg)
Elevation	45–80 degrees
Traverse	7 to 21 degrees depending upon elevation
Weight of bomb	20lb (9.07kg) (streamlined); 20.5lb (9.30kg) (cylindrical)
Maximum range	4,100yd (3,750m) (streamlined); 3,250yd (2,972m) (cylindrical)
Rate of fire	18rd/min

The 4.2in mortar was originally designed early in 1941 to meet a General Staff requirement for a chemical warfare mortar which could fire a high-explosive (HE) bomb in a subsidiary role as well as for ranging purposes. Its eventual appearance as an infantry mortar was the result of a demand from the C-in-C Middle East in November 1931 for a mortar capable of out-ranging the German and Italian opposition, specifying that it must have a range in excess of 4,400yd. Eyes were directed to the chemical mortar, a new streamlined HE bomb was quickly designed, and by the spring of 1942 the design had been approved and had passed its safety tests.

The design was little more than a scaled-up 3in, using the same sort of barrel, bipod and baseplate configuration, suitably enlarged and strengthened to fire the heavier bomb. Consequently, the result was a very heavy mortar which could only be carried by a tracked vehicle, was slow and cumbersome to bring into and out of action, and imposed a heavy logistic load on the infantry battalion. It was, therefore, issued to the units who were originally set up to fire them as chemical warfare weapons, the mortar companies of the Royal Engineers. The mortar eventually finished up in the Royal Artillery. In this original form it saw limited use, principally in the Far East where it was man-carried through the jungle.

The mortar was provided with two bombs, a streamlined HE and a cylindrical HE, the latter carrying more payload but having less range. The propelling charge was a single primary cartridge in the tail unit, with six secondaries in celluloid tubes fitted between the fins and retained by a spring.

A rare picture of the original British Mark 1 4.2in mortar in action, probably in North Africa. Note that they are firing the early cylindrical bomb.

Ordnance, ML, SB, 4.2in Mortar Mark 2

Calibre	4.2in (107mm)
Barrel length	68.28in (1.734m)
Weight in action	907lb (411kg)

Other details as for Mark 1 (*see previous page*).

The 4.2in Mark 2 mortar on its mobile baseplate; the mortar has obviously not fired, since the baseplate has not bedded into the ground.

The Mark 2 was the same mortar as the Mark 1 but with a heavier baseplate with wheels, allowing the entire equipment to be towed behind more or less any light vehicle. It could be brought into action very rapidly by simply unlocking the suspension units and rotating the wheels so as to drop the baseplate to the ground. The barrel and bipod were carried clamped to the baseplate and were then removed, the barrel inserted into the rebound socket and the bipod fitted to it. A quasi-optical collimating sight was fitted, together with an elevating level.

Ammunition available included the same two HE bombs which had been developed for the Mark 1 mortar, plus a cylindrical smoke bomb which was provided with various fillings. White phosphorus was the normal smoke filling, but for situations where the fire risk from phosphorus was hazardous or tactically undesirable, FM (titanium tetrachloride) or CSAM (chlorsulphonic acid mixture) could be supplied. In later years a discarding sabot bomb was developed in order to provide a base ejection smoke bomb using the standard HC mixture. The ballistic performance remained the same as that of the Mark 1 mortar. The Mark 2 remained in service until the early 1960s.

A 4.2in mortar of 383 Light Battery RA(TA) at practice on Salisbury Plain in 1954.

The 4.2in mortars of 40th Infantry Division on parade in Hong Kong, 1949.

The Blacker Bombard, a spigot mortar firing a heavy bomb as an anti-tank weapon. This is the Bombard on its ground mount, but most were placed on concrete cylinders to cover roadblocks; the cylinders, identifiable by the stainless-steel pivot pin in the top centre, can still be found in a few wartime sites which have remained undisturbed.

in 1941–2 designs for an alternative 4in model were put in hand as a form of insurance in case the 4.2in failed to make the grade. A design was produced in prototype form and some bombs were made and fired, but before much more could be done the 4.2in mortar's troubles were all solved and consequently the work on the 4in was stopped. Thirty years later, somebody discovered that, by some sort of departmental oversight, the design of high-explosive bomb for this 4in mortar had been officially introduced during the trials but had never been officially declared obsolete when the development stopped. In order to keep the records straight, a notice of obsoletion was forthwith published, which caused a good deal of head-scratching and searching through files by people who had never even known that it existed.

Probably the most all-embracing and ingenious proposition of all was one put up by a former employee of the Skoda Works in Pilsen, Czechoslovakia, who had escaped to Britain and joined the British Army. He proposed a multi-purpose mortar which, according to his description, would fire '2in mortar bombs, No. 36

grenades, German 5cm bombs, and all types of spigot bomb.' While his idea was commended for its ingenuity, it was felt that there was no requirement for such a device and it was reluctantly declined. Unfortunately, I have never been able to trace any drawings of this weapon, so I am therefore unable to explain how it managed to achieve its advertised functions.

BLACKER AND HIS BOMBARD

In 1940 the British Army scraped home from the continent of Europe, having left almost all of its equipment behind, and set about organizing itself against a probable invasion by the German Army. At the same time, the Home Guard was set up as a form of third-line defence against invasion and, having been set up, it had to be armed. Airfields had to be defended; roadblocks had to be prepared; defensive lines of pillboxes needed to be given weapons capable of stopping the dreaded Panzers. Into this void came weapons inventors, many of them with very little knowledge or experience of weapons, offering cheap and quick solutions. One of the few who managed to get a hearing was Lt Col Blacker, who produced another of his spigot mortar designs. This was mounted on top of a concrete cylinder and could be traversed in any direction with the aid of a pair of bicycle handlebars. The barrel was large but was merely a shroud surrounding the central spigot, a 29mm (1.1in) diameter rod. The bomb had a bulbous nose and a long tail tube ending in a set of fins, and inside this tail tube was a cartridge and a percussion cap. The spigot contained a firing pin, controlled by a lever on the handlebars. The whole thing was crowned by a very primitive sight that catered for moving targets. This was the 'Blacker Bombard' and it formed a major support weapon for the Home Guard and was also used for the defence of airfields and similar vulnerable points by the regular forces. The bomb weighed 20lb (9kg) and the weapon had a range of about 100yd (90m).

Firing the 10cm Nebelwerfer 35, the German gas and smoke mortar, which, like all the others of its type, became a normal mortar firing HE bombs.

NO SMOKE WITHOUT FIRE

The German Army also took steps to produce a chemical warfare potential using a medium calibre mortar, with the formation of Nebeltruppen, or Smoke Troops. Their function was to provide smoke screens for tactical use and also, should the occasion arise, to be able to deliver gas, using their 10cm calibre Nebelwefer or smoke mortar. As with the Americans and British, the Germans insured against under-employment of the specialized troops by developing a high-explosive bomb for use with the Nebelwerfer and, of course, this turned out to be more widely used during the war than the original smoke armament while, as with other combatants, the gas projectiles were never used.

The Nebeltruppen and their Nebelwerfers also acted as a most convenient 'front' for a weapon which was to remain a close secret until it was deployed against the Russians in late 1941 – the field rocket projector. It was a nine-barrel lightweight wheeled launcher which fired nine

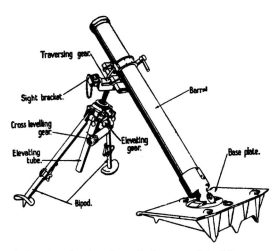

A drawing showing the main features of the 10cm NbW 35, which appeared in a British Army pamphlet Notes on Enemy Weapons *in 1942.*

substantial 15cm spin-stabilized rockets in quick succession, a most formidable and awe-inspiring weapon, and it was officially known as the 15cm Nebelwerfer 41. Giving it this misleading title meant that anyone not 'in the know' who heard it

The 15cm Nebelwerfer 41 was an entirely different weapon but used the Nebelwerfer name simply to conceal its real system of operation – a smokescreen, you might say. This was a multiple-barrelled rocket projector which fired a 32kg (76lb) rocket to over 7,000m (7,660yd) range.

The German 5cm Granatwerfer 36; the heavy baseplate and intricate controls made for accuracy at the expense of weight.

Firing the 5cm GrW 36 was a two-man job – one to load and the other to aim.

The 8cm (actually 81mm) Granatwerfer 34, which was the standard German Army company mortar and the one most frequently encountered.

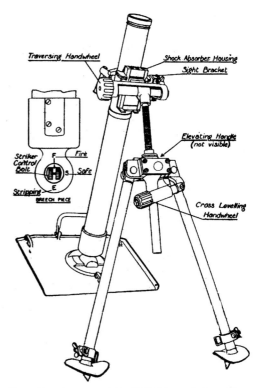

The salient features of the GrW 34, again from Notes on Enemy Weapons.

mentioned would simply assume it to be another smoke mortar and not worth any consideration.

WORLD WAR II

When the war broke out in 1939 the line-up of the mortars of the principal nations was more or less similar. The British had their 2in, ranging to 500yd (457m) with a 2lb bomb, as an infantry platoon weapon, with the 3in firing a 10lb (4.5kg) bomb to 1,600yd (1,460m) as the company support mortar. The 4.2in, which was to fire a 20lb (9kg) bomb to 4,000yd (3,660m), was still under development at this time and, in any case, was intended for chemical warfare.

The German Army had the Granatwerfer 36 of 5cm calibre, equivalent to the British 2in

German 81mm

8cm Granatwerfer 34

Calibre	81.4mm (3.18in)
Barrel length	1.143m (45in)
Weight in action	56kg (124lb)
Elevation	40–90 degrees
Traverse	9–15 degrees, dependent upon elevation
Projectile weight	3.42kg (7.5lb)
Maximum range	2,400m (2,625yd)
Rate of fire	15rd/min

The 8cm Schwere Granatwerfer 34 was a conventional design of mortar, based on the Stokes pattern but with a few native variations. It was standard equipment in all rifle companies, two mortars being held in the Granatwerfergruppe. On the march the mortar was usually carried in a light horse-drawn cart, one member of the detachment being described in the establishment as the Pferdführer or 'horse-leader'. In action, the three basic sections, barrel, baseplate and bipod, were carried by the members of the detachment, together with twenty-one rounds of ammunition.

The GrW 34 was provided with a range of ammunition which included two remarkable bombs, the Wurfgranaten 38 and 39. These were 'bouncing bombs' which were intended to produce an airburst effect at the target. The 'approved' method of obtaining airbursts is, of course, to provide the bombs with a time fuze, but this means calculation of the necessary time of flight and the setting of each fuze before firing, a time-

The original 8cm Granatwerfer 34 seen from the front; note the cross-level control is at the top of the bipod.

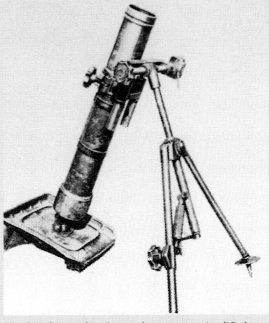

The 8cm Stummelwerfer, or short mortar, simplified manufacture by putting the cross-level at the bottom of the bipod, operating on the bottom of the elevating standard.

German 81mm *continued*

consuming exercise which has no place in an infantry mortar's operation. The 'bouncing bomb' resembled a normal bomb in appearance, but instead of the bomb body being a solid casting, the head was separate and pinned to the rest of the body. The body proper terminated in a flat head containing a channel filled with gunpowder, and the space within the head carried a charge of smokeless powder. An impact fuze was fitted in the nose. When the bomb landed at the target, this impact fuse ignited the smokeless powder, which exploded. The explosion blew the body back up into the air and detonated the bomb when it was some 15 to 20ft above the ground, thus showering the area with fragments.

The rebound action was, of course, highly dependent upon the nature of the ground at the target; if it were soft, the explosion might well blow the nose into the ground instead of sending the body into the air. But on any firm surface it was quite effective. A copy was later developed in Britain for the 3in mortar, but its erratic behaviour on soft ground led to the idea being dropped.

Variant

8cm Kurz GrW 42 or Stummelwerfer. This was a shortened lightweight version; it used the same ammunition but had the barrel length reduced to 747mm (29.4in), and had the baseplate and bipod lightened and simplified. The total weight was reduced to 28.1kg (62lb) and the maximum range dropped to 1,100m (1,200yd). Originally developed for airborne troops, it was later taken into use by all infantry and largely replaced the standard model. The loss of range was compensated for by easier handling.

German 12cm Heavy

Schwere 12cm Granatwerfer 42

Calibre	120mm (4.68in)
Barrel length	1.875m (73.8in)
Weight in action	285kg (628lb)
Elevation	45–84 degrees
Traverse	8–16 degrees, varying with elevation
Weight of bomb	15.8kg (34.84lb)
Maximum range	6,050m (6,620yds)
Rate of fire	15rd/min

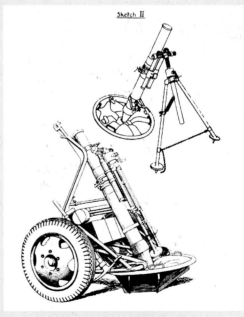

In the early days of its advance against Russia in 1941, the German Army captured vast quantities of artillery material, much of which was put to use against its former owners. Among this booty were large numbers of the 12cm Soviet mortar model 1938; in Soviet hands this was an artillery weapon, but the German Army issued it as an infantry mortar under the nomenclature GrW 378(r). It was successful and well-liked by its new operators, and as a result it was decided to manufacture a German copy, which was issued late in 1942 as the GrW 42. There were some small differences in the German design, both to improve the weapon and to facilitate manufacture by German methods. The maximum elevation of the Russian weapon was only

The first Allied intimation of the German 120mm mortar came in an intelligence report in 1943.

German 12cm Heavy *continued*

This appears to be an originally Russian mortar adapted to German sights by the addition of a peculiar bracket.

The bigger the mortar the more complicated laying it becomes; this is a three-man effort, one for line, one for elevation and, over his shoulder, the cross-level man.

80 degrees and the traverse 8 to 14 degrees; these were increased. The track of the transporter was increased in width for better stability in towing, and the baseplate, bipod and transporter were made rather more robust and thus somewhat heavier – a total weight increase of about 45kg (100lb) in the transit mode.

The design of the mortar was quite conventional. A smooth-bore barrel was locked into a circular baseplate and supported by a bipod with a two-spring shock absorber unit connecting the barrel and bipod together. For movement, a transporter was provided; this was a framework of steel tubing carrying two short axles on which were mounted pressed-steel wheels (perforated in the German model, plain in the Russian) with pneumatic tyres. A towing eye at the front end allowed it to be pulled by any convenient vehicle. At the front end of the framework was a circular clamp to hold the mortar barrel, and the rear end was formed into a U-shape which fitted into two brackets on the baseplate of the mortar.

To bring the mortar out of action, all that was necessary was to lift the bipod out of the ground, bring the mortar barrel vertical and swing the bipod around it so that it lay, folded, at the rear of the barrel, and then push the transporter into position with its frame vertical so that the U-brackets locked into the baseplate. The barrel was then pushed forward until it lay in the barrel clamp, where it was secured, and the bipod feet were strapped to a bracket on the frame. By pulling the towing eye downwards, leverage was applied which would lift the baseplate from the ground and the unit was ready to travel. Bringing the mortar into action was simply the reverse process.

tactically, firing a 0.9kg (2lb) bomb to 500m (550yd); it was much more complicated and heavy than the British model – it weighed 14kg (31lb) as against 8.5kg (19lb) – but had the edge in accuracy. The company weapon was the 8cm Granatwerfer 34, firing a 0.5kg (1.1lb) bomb to 2,400m (2,625m); it thus had greater range than the British 3in but delivered a lighter bomb. The

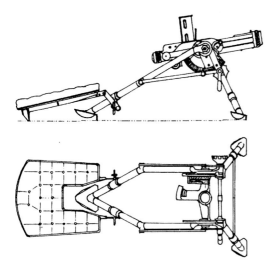

A drawing of the Italian Mortiao d'Assalto e Accompagnamento Brixia 45 Mod 35. The lower plan view had the barrel removed so as to reveal the mounting details.

An Italian team at work with the 45mm Brixia mortar. The man lying on the padded frame operates the breech, while the second man drops the bombs in and the NCO spots the fall of shot.

The Brandt 60mm mortar looked the same wherever it appeared; the French Mle 35 was exactly like this American M42.

Nebeltruppen had the 10cm Nebelwerfer 35, a conventional mortar that fired a 7.3kg (16lb) bomb to 3,000m (3,300yd), and, of course, they also had their rocket-launcher in the final stages of development and, as we shall see, were also about to receive a most complicated replacement for the 10cm 35.

The Italian Army had the 45mm Model 35, an odd-looking weapon mounted on a tripod-cum-baseplate on which the operator could either sit or lie. It was breech-loaded, by pulling a handle to withdraw the lower part of the barrel from the upper and thus leave a gap into which a bomb could be dropped, and the breech section also included a gas-port system. There was also the 81mm Mortiao 35, which was a Brandt derivative identical to the American 81mm M1 and fired similar bombs.

France, of course, was equipped entirely with Brandt designs, from the 50mm Lance Grenades Modèle 37 which was the platoon weapon and had replaced the rifle grenade, then to the 60mm Mortier Modèle 35 and finally the 81mm Mortier Modèle 31. The 60mm and 81mm were standard Brandt and were also widely used elsewhere – the

USA and Italy most prominently – and were quite conventional drop-fired weapons sending a 1.3kg (2.8lb) 60mm bomb to 1,700m (1,860yd) and a 3.3kg (7.2lb) 81mm bomb to 2,850m (3,120yd). Both complicated the issue by having light and heavy bombs; this was a popular pre-war practice since it offered greater range for far-out harassment or greater destructive power for close-in protection, but in real life it was found to be an irritation. The bomb you wanted was never the one you had, and most armies began to abandon the heavy bomb and use the light one for all tasks, primarily because they saw range as being the more important and, of course, the infantryman could carry more light bombs than heavy ones, and he could also load and fire them faster when the need arose.

Further afield, both the Russian Army and the Japanese Army fielded a surprising collection of mortars. The Russian armoury began at platoon level with a collection of 50mm mortars of various sorts, the result of a progressive series of models, each getting rid of another objection from the users. Bear in mind that the USSR spent more of its gross domestic product on armament than any other nation on earth at that time, and had sufficient money available to allow three or four competing designs to be produced in quite large quantities so that thorough testing in the hands of troops could eliminate the weaklings. The Russian infantry platoons had originally, in the early 1930s, been given a unique 'spade mortar' of 37mm calibre. It looked like a spade and you could actually dig with it – the handle was the barrel and it fitted into the socket of a spade blade. By separating the two, removing a single support strut from inside the barrel, and then coupling the base of the barrel into a special socket in the centre of the blade, it turned into a questionably efficient mortar capable of firing a 0.7kg (1.5lb) bomb to about 275m (300yd).

It seems that the infantry were less than impressed by this offering and in 1938 a 'proper' 50mm mortar appeared. This time the designers had gone too far in the other direction and produced an over-complicated weapon in the belief that they were making things simpler for the soldier. The mortar was designed so that it could be locked at two elevations only – 45 degrees and 75 degrees – and range adjustment was done by turning a slipping ring around the lower end of the barrel so as to expose gas escape holes. This permitted some of the propelling charge gas to be wasted to the outside air and thus reduced the range. This gave a maximum range of

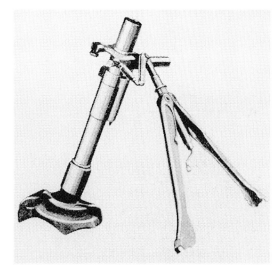

The Russian PM-40 was largely made of stamped or drawn steel and was restricted to two elevations.

The PM-41 was aimed at simplifying production and was an ingenious design, though still restricted to two elevations.

800m (875yd) with a 0.8kg (1.9lb) bomb, but trying to remember the correct combinations of elevation and gas port opening for different ranges in the heat of battle must have been very difficult.

In the event, the M1938 mortar turned out to be too expensive to manufacture, and it was rapidly supplanted by the M1939; this was more or less the same but did away with the gas ports and fixed elevations in favour of a conventional screw elevating gear. The performance remained the same. It, too, met with disapproval when the cost was worked out, and the M1940 was quickly designed to replace it. This had a stamped steel baseplate, a stamped steel bipod, a drawn tube barrel, but reverted to the two-elevation and gas port system of the M1938. But apparently the operating rules were simplified, and this became popular and widely used throughout the war.

Red Army soldiers with the PM-41 mortar on backpacks. The German invasion in 1941 cut short the production of this model in favour of other weapons which were more vital.

The 82mm Model 43 introduced the idea of using wheels instead of the bipod to support the elevating apparatus. Note the firing supports beneath the wheels.

Finally, there came a 50mm Model 1941 in which ease of mass-production had obviously been at the forefront of the designer's mind. Instead of a bipod the barrel was supported in a yoke attached to the baseplate, which gave the requisite degree of traverse and the two fixed elevations. The gas port system of range control was continued but instead of merely allowing the gas to escape at the breech end, it was vented forwards in a tube beneath the barrel. The whole thing folded up very neatly and could be carried on a special backpack, but it is not believed that many were manufactured. It was introduced just before the German invasion and it seems that production was curtailed; there were sufficient of the M1940 for the army's needs and there were other, more vital weapons, demanding factory space, so the M1941 mortar was shelved.

The company mortar was another copy of the French Brandt design, but in 82mm calibre, in order to follow the usual Soviet practice of using calibres close to the norm but sufficiently different to prevent enemies from using Soviet ammunition in their weapons or Soviet weapons with non-Soviet ammunition. The 82mm M1936 fired a 3.4kg (7.5lb) bomb to 3,020m (3,300yd), a performance that was slightly better than most 81mm weapons and which thus showed another Soviet characteristic, that of shaving the factor of safety rather lower than was accepted in western nations so as to extract just that little bit more performance. This was gradually improved; in 1941 a new model appeared which pioneered the idea of using a pair of wheels and an axle to support the barrel instead of the conventional bipod or tripod. The barrel sat in the usual circular baseplate, but attached to the lower end of the barrel were two arms, each with a stub axle and wheel. A muzzle cap with two handles locked on to the end of the barrel so that it could be pulled along by two men; there were also handles on the baseplate so that the rest of the crew could lend a hand when the going got sticky. To put the mortar into action, they merely tipped it back until the baseplate was on the ground; the two legs with the wheels stuck out in front and gave the necessary support to the barrel.

This looked very neat and efficient, but in fact the balancing act was a little too finely tuned, and the designer had also overlooked what happened as the baseplate sank into the ground under prolonged firing while the wheels and arms stayed on top; after a time it became rather difficult to reach lower angles of elevation, and eventually the mortar would fall over backwards. So the design was replaced by a much improved model in which the wheels were attached to a normal axle, and from the centre of the axle there rose an elevating standard which was attached to the usual sort of barrel collar. As before, there was a muzzle cap arranged for pulling, and in transport the tube lay across the axle, held in a clamp which was part of the elevating standard. There was also a bracket that held two shoes positioned behind the wheels. On arriving at the firing position the barrel was tipped up so that the baseplate hit the ground, the clamp was undone and the wheels were run forward. This caused the barrel standard fitting to revolve around the axle

Loading the 107mm M38 mortar somewhere in Siberia.

so that the two shoes hit the ground and, when the wheels were heaved forward, slipped beneath the wheels to act as firing supports. When the mortar was elevated – by screwing out the central stem of the elevating standard – the collar would slide up and down the barrel while also carrying the traversing screw mechanism and sight. It was an ingenious design which stayed in service for many years after the war, and which, one surmises, was given a long and hard look by Hotchkiss-Brandt when the company started on its 120mm design in post-war years.

The next step in calibre was rather odd – 107mm. This is, of course, 4.2in, and it appeared at much the same time as weapons of the same calibre appeared in US and UK development programmes. It is the only known case of the Soviets adopting a calibre in use in the West, perhaps because they thought that since the American mortar was rifled there could be no interchangeability of ammunition, and so their

A group of Soviet 107mm mortars in action; note the man on the forward crest with an observing instrument, directing the fire.

Laying the Soviet 120mm heavy battalion mortar.

The Soviet 120mm mortar in march order, during post-war trials in the USA.

security was still inviolate. The Model 38 was apparently intended as the support mortar for mountain troops, the theory being, presumably, that if soldiers were going to have to cart a mortar up the side of a mountain they might just as well cart one with a sizeable bomb to make the endeavour worthwhile. It fired an 8kg (17.6lb) bomb to 5,760m (6,300yd), comfortably outperforming both the US and UK 4.2in models, and did it in an overall weight of 170kg (375lb), which, again, suggests that the factor of safety had been very carefully shaved.

The Red Army, however, had a further surprise up its sleeve; it also had a 120mm *regimental* mortar, a solid weapon which was taken into action on a wheeled carriage, from which the conventional sort of baseplate, bipod and barrel were unloaded and set up. It fired a 6.8kg (15lb) bomb to 6,000m (6,500yd) and was introduced into service in 1938, though nobody outside Russia knew of it until 1941.

THE KNEE MORTAR – AND OTHERS

The Japanese were early mortar enthusiasts, adopting a 50mm 'grenade launcher' in 1921. This was the Type 10, a short-barrelled mortar but with the barrel mounted on a short support rod attached to the baseplate. A gas escape ring was used to vary the range, and the mortar, of course, had infinitely variable elevation and was fired by a lanyard. It used the standard Model 91 hand grenade as a projectile but also had pyrotechnic, and smoke bombs provided.

It was replaced in 1929 by the Type 89, a most remarkable little weapon. At first glance it looked exactly like the Type 10 but it had one significant difference: the firing pin was mounted on a threaded stalk, which was also the supporting rod, and the barrel could be screwed up and down on this rod. This action caused the firing pin to protrude into the barrel for a greater or lesser distance, and the greater the distance it intruded, the greater the space behind the bomb when it was fired. And this space had to be filled with gas before the bomb took off, so that screwing the barrel up and down the firing pin rod gave very precise control of the propelling charge power and thus the range for any elevation.

This mortar fired the same grenade as the earlier model, but also had a specially designed projectile which was quite unlike any other mortar bomb. Shaped like an artillery shell, it had a copper sealing ring around the rear end and a number of holes in the base, sealed with varnished paper. In the centre of the base was a percussion cap. The rear end was, in fact, a propellant chamber and held a charge of smokeless powder, so that when the bomb was dropped into the mortar and the firing pin tripped, the cap fired the powder and the resulting gases blew through the holes and into the chamber space behind the bomb and so produced the necessary pressure to launch it. In addition, there was a row of small holes underneath the copper sealing ring, and the pressure also blew through those and forced the sealing ring tight against the barrel so as to effectively trap the propelling gas behind the bomb for greater efficiency.

The mortar was popular, and in every platoon there was one man who carried it, strapped to his leg for convenience – it weighed only 10lb. Unfortunately, this led to it being referred to in documents as the 'Leg Mortar'. Even more unfortunately, some translator, working on captured Japanese documents, translated this as 'knee mortar'. And because the curved baseplate just fitted nicely on the curve of the thigh, several Allied soldiers assumed that, being strong and fit, they could kneel down on one knee, plant the baseplate on the raised thigh, and fire the mortar. It could be done – once. After that he was on the ground with a compound fracture of the upper thigh; there was never a chance of a second shot.

The Japanese also deployed another peculiar 50mm mortar, the Type 98. This was intended solely as a demolition device, and it fired an ungainly projectile which was no more than a square box loaded with slabs of picric acid and attached to the end of a 50mm diameter stick. The mortar was set up at a fixed 45-degree elevation, a gunpowder charge was loaded, and the bomb stick was inserted to a distance pre-set by a sliding range gauge below the muzzle. This was positioned to the required range and the end of the scale protruded beyond the mortar muzzle so that the body of the bomb rested on it, so limiting the distance that the stick entered into the barrel. The range was thus governed by the amount of free space in the mortar which had to be filled up with gas before the bomb started to move. The bomb weighed 14lb (6kg), and the maximum range was 450yd (410m); on landing, the picric acid produced an enormous amount of blast, enabling the mortar to be used for removing field defences. Some wartime documents claim that it could also fire Bangalore torpedoes, but this looks like another mistranslation; the Japanese Bangalore torpedo was 52in long and about 35mm in diameter, and firing that out of a 50mm mortar with a barrel 25in long would have been an interesting ballistic proposition, to say the least.

The Japanese adopted the familiar 81mm Brandt as their company mortar in 1928, then obtained a licence and put it into production at Yokosuka Naval Arsenal as the Type 3. And although it was later augmented by improved models, it remained in production until 1943. Nevertheless, they were not very impressed by its performance – it fired the customary light and heavy bombs, to a maximum range of about 3,000yd (2,745m) with the light bomb – and set about improving it by tightening up the tolerances of bore and bomb diameters. By reducing the windage, less gas was wasted in blow-by, the bomb was more stable, and both range and accuracy were improved, the range going up to 3,250yd (2,970m). This went into production as the Type 97 in 1937, and was simply a new barrel on the same Type 3 baseplate and bipod, together with better ammunition.

The only fault the army could find with the Type 97 was that it was a bit too cumbersome to be rushed around the battlefield by half-a-dozen men; the whole thing weighed about 145lb (65kg) and the barrel was just over 4ft (1,220mm) long. Something more compact was desirable, and hence a new 81mm 'small mortar Type 99' appeared in 1939. This was just a simplified and short-barrelled version of the Type 97, firing the same ammunition, the principal advantage being that the weight was reduced to about 55lb (25kg). The performance, of course, suffered – the maximum range came down to 2,200yd (2,010m) – but the advantages outweighed the drawbacks

and the small mortar became the preferred model throughout the war.

The Japanese armoury was rounded off by two 90mm mortars, heavy weapons fitted with recoil absorbing mountings and firing a 12lb (5.4kg) bomb to 4,100yd (3,750m), and a 150mm Type 97 which fired a 57lb (26kg) bomb to 2,200yd. This latter weapon, though, weighed over 700lb (320kg) – almost one-third of a ton – which was not really the optimum for mobile warfare, and was rarely encountered during the war.

IMPROVING THE MORTAR

One of the drawbacks that the mortar had to overcome in 1939 was the legacy of World War I inherent in the title: people were still calling it a '*trench* mortar'; indeed, this was a common failing in Britain and France in 1939–40 that people were still referring to the front line as 'the trenches' when they were nothing of the sort. It was all part of what appears to have been a subconscious belief that things were going to be picked up where they had left off in 1918 and played by the same rules, which is why the events of May and June 1940 came as such a traumatic shock. And because of this 'trench' mentality, there were many who found it difficult to visualize a role for the mortar if there were no trenches. The Germans, and to a lesser extent the Japanese due to their prolonged 'Manchurian Incident', had worked out a suitable role for the infantry support weapon, sufficient to demonstrate to their opponents that there quite definitely was a place for mortars in fluid warfare. The trouble was that so long as the word 'trench' had any currency, there seemed little incitement to develop the mortar to fire at long ranges; everybody knew that trenches were only a few hundred yards apart, and provided you could get the bomb across no man's land and into the rear supply trenches, that was all that was needed. But if the mortar was to be of any use in mobile warfare then it had to have more range, so that the target was not constantly moving out of range and the mortar therefore constantly having to be shifted. There is an old maxim among artillerymen that 'guns on wheels are useless', which is not, as some think, an attack on self-propulsion, but a truism pointing out that a gun cannot be used when it is in the process of moving. By the end of 1940 the infantry were beginning to see the truth of that little maxim, and were beginning to ask for more range.

There is, of course, nothing inherently difficult in giving any weapon more range; you simply increase the length of the barrel and/or the size of the cartridge. But when you are dealing with a man-portable weapon, this rule of thumb has to be abandoned, because whichever combination you choose means more weight on the soldier's back. The only way to obtain more range is to completely redesign the weapon using stronger materials, so that the explosive force of a more powerful propelling charge can be safely contained in a stronger barrel, for example. This does tend to lead to a modest increase in weight, but it is usually acceptable; unfortunately, in the early 1940s there was another ingrained belief about mortars – that they were cheap, easily made, and fired cheap, easily made ammunition. But as soon as there were specifications for high-yield steel for mortar barrels and high-strength light alloys for baseplates, the 'cheap' aspect went straight into the discard.

The British Army solved the problem in a very practical manner; a 3in mortar was taken out to a proof range and fired with gradually increasing charges until the barrel began showing signs of distress, whereupon the army went back to the previous charge and settled for that. This increased the maximum range from 1,600 to 2,800yd (1,460–2,560m), but the baseplate had to be strengthened to take the heavier blow without buckling. It was also found that mortar usage was becoming so great that it was necessary to build a complete new explosives factory at Powfoot, Scotland, which did nothing but make mortar cartridges.

By 1943, though, the army was back again, asking for more range, and the designers had to bite the bullet and develop a new barrel. They adopted 45-ton steel, instead of the previous 34-ton (these figures being a measure of the breaking strain during testing), but firing increased charges made the barrels bulge. The army had not specified any particular range; it was merely asking for as much range as possible consistent with accuracy, so the designers tried again, this time with a 50-ton steel for the barrels. With this, they were able to reach 3,500yd (3,200m), but the accuracy was not acceptable and the whole project was abandoned. The Canadian Army then tried its hand, designing a new barrel which was 30in (760mm) longer than normal. All this achieved was a 300yd (275m) increase in range for a 32lb (14.5kg) increase in weight, so that idea was also discarded.

By this time, the 4.2in mortar had gone into service, but although 4,000yd (3,660m) had been promised, it was found that the baseplate would not stand the recoil from a charge sufficient to send the early patterns of bomb to this range, and the range was restricted to 3,300yd (3,020m) until a new pattern of lighter bomb could be provided. One of the greatest difficulties with this mortar was the weight of the component parts, which made it rather an unpleasant article to man-pack. Hence it was generally dismantled and strapped to a tracked 'universal carrier' or the bits thrown into a trailer behind a jeep.

The problem was eventually solved by producing a wheeled baseplate of ingenious design. Two wheels were carried on swinging axle arms on either side of the baseplate. For travelling, these arms were locked so as to carry the baseplate with adequate ground clearance, and the mortar barrel and bipod were strapped on top of the baseplate. To drop into action, the locking pins of the axle arms were pulled out, allowing the baseplate to drop to the ground and the wheels to 'float' on the surface of the ground. The breech-piece of the mortar fitted into a quick release stud in the baseplate, the bipod unit slipped over the barrel, and there it was, ready to fire in a matter of seconds. As the weapon was fired, the baseplate tended to bury itself in the ground, but the wheels merely rested on the surface, the axle arms allowing relative movement between the two. When ready to come out of action, the barrel and bipod were stripped down and strapped to the baseplate in the travelling mode, and then two handspikes, those favourite standbys of all gunners, were inserted into the axle arms. One good heave and the action of the handspikes and axle arms levered the baseplate out of the ground and up onto its wheels once more, ready to travel. It was possible for a well-trained detachment to drop the mortar into action, fire twenty bombs, pack up and be gone from the position before the last bomb had landed on the target. This sort of shoot-and-scoot technique made sure that any retaliatory fire landed in thin air so far as the mortar men were concerned, although it did not help to make friends among the people who occupied the adjacent areas and who had to sit there and take what was intended for the now-absent mortars. Moreover, the early wartime production of the bomb tail units was a bit slapdash, and it was not entirely unknown for a tail to part company with the bomb shortly after it left the mortar, so that the bomb was wildly unstable and, after turning end over end a few times, would land within a couple of hundred yards. Since this often meant it was landing on the friendly side of the front instead of the hostile one, it was little wonder that some occupants of the forward area were less than pleased when they saw a 4.2in mortar approaching.

On the other hand, the weapon did some sterling work. In Burma, where artillery activities were considerably restricted by the jungle terrain, some artillery regiments were converted to 4.2in mortar regiments, and with artillery fire-control techniques grafted onto the fast reaction time of the mortar, and the high lethality coefficient of the bomb, they were probably more useful in that particular theatre than more conventional guns

would have been. At least one unit was manned by West African troops who were in the habit of head-carrying their mortars through the jungle, which virtually meant that anywhere a man could walk, artillery could go.

AMERICAN MORTARS – A SHAKY START

In the US Army the 60mm and 81mm mortars stayed the course with relatively small changes, and it was the erstwhile chemical weapon which came to its fulfilment during the war. Once the USA entered the war, and indeed some time before, due to the activities of the British Army and the German Army being closely followed by the more percipient US Army officers, the need for a medium-range infantry support weapon had become evident, and eventually Gen Porter, then Chief of the Chemical Warfare Service, put forward the suggestion to standardize the design of the high-explosive 4.2in mortar shell which had been perfected, and offered the services of chemical mortar units as infantry support troops, since it appeared that there would be little call for their primary task of firing gas shells, and restricting their activities to smoke-screening operations would have been a waste of valuable manpower and weapons. After discussions between Gen Porter and Gen Marshall, Army Chief of Staff, the suggestion was approved in principle, and steps were taken to authorize the provision of mortars and ammunition. However, mere approval at the top was not enough. The War Department now had to modify its tactical doctrines to accommodate the new weapon and, probably the greatest task, the rest of the army had to be convinced that the idea made sense. In February 1943 a conference was held to explain the new role of the 4.2in mortar, but the Army Ground Forces were unconvinced; they suggested that the weapon ought to go to the field artillery for use as a light support weapon in substitution for the 105mm howitzer in theatres which were

US 4.2in

Mortar, Chemical, 4.2in M2

Calibre	4.2in (107mm)
Barrel length	48in (1.22m), rifled, 24 grooves, rh, one turn in 20 calibres
Weight in action	335lb (152kg)
Elevation	45–60 degrees
Traverse	8 degrees left or right
Projectiles	24.5lb (11.11kg)
Maximum range	4,357yd (4,000m)
Rate of fire	20rd/min

As related earlier in this chaper, this first appeared in the 1920s but had been sidelined during the 1930s as being a purely chemical warfare weapon. The US Chemical Warfare Service, however, quietly developed a high-explosive bomb and when, in 1942, the need for a powerful mortar became pressing, it was ready with the answer. This weapon was to see considerable service during World War II and continued in use, with a revised and improved model appearing in the 1960s, until the middle 1980s. It is still in use in Greece and several other countries.

The principal feature is the rifling, and the consequent spin-stabilized ammunition. The projectile is square-based like an artillery shell and can use standard artillery fuzes. There is a centrally located, perforated cylindrical cartridge holder in the base of the shell, inside which is the usual primary cartridge and outside which are the secondary charges in the form of bundles of sheet propellant with a hole punched in the middle and a slot in one side, so that they can be slipped around the cartridge container tube. The copper driving ring is a prominent feature of all the projectiles.

The mortar is of otherwise conventional style, though not conventional in form. The baseplate was

A 4.2inch M1 in action in Italy, 1944.

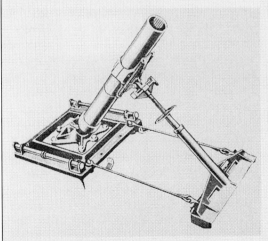

The US 4.2in M1 was quite unique in its construction, using a single standard instead of a bipod and linking it to the baseplate.

US 4.2in *continued*

rectangular, with four built-in telescoping carrying handles, one at each corner. The barrel had the usual separate breech-piece screwed on, with a fixed firing pin. Instead of a bipod, there was a 'standard', a single tube containing a shock-absorbing mechanism, and the screw elevating mechanism, at the top of which was the traversing screw and a barrel collar with more shock-absorbing springs. At the foot of the standard was a wide spade-like shoe, linked to the front corners of the baseplate by steel tie-rods. This method of construction gave a very stable mortar but restricted the elevation to 60 degrees.

---

short of that weapon. The arguments were long and hard, but in the end the CWS's point of view was accepted, and on 19 March 1943 the 4.2in mortar was officially approved as a high-explosive-firing support weapon.

Finally came the task of selling the new weapon to the commanders in the field. Their previous contact with the CWS had been relatively small, and the general impression was that they were a corps of scientific bent, concerned with gas masks and gas attacks rather than with more formal methods of combat. Eventually though, after some active propaganda by the CWS higher command, the word got through that this new addition to the teeth of the army might not be such a bad idea after all.

When the USA entered the war there were but four mortar companies in existence, and one of these was lost at Bataan, while another was deactivated early in 1942. In the late spring of 1942 four more were activated to bring the total to six, but there the strength rested until May 1943, since nothing more than gas and smoke missions were envisaged for them and it was believed that there would be none of the former and little of the latter to justify any great expansion of the service.

This, of course, led to embarrassment all round when the propagandizing began to take effect; after being convinced of the utility of a chemical mortar company, numerous commanders began demanding provision of such units for their commands, to a point where the demand far exceeded the supply. The CWS made urgent noises and requested permission to form another nineteen units, but things moved slowly. Then

came the breakthrough; four battalions were ordered to take part in the invasion of Sicily. To replace them in the USA four more were authorized to be formed, and once the reports from Sicily were received and studied, more units began to be put together and trained.

In the invasion of Sicily the mortars had proved their worth; moreover, with over a thousand men in a battalion there was sufficient manpower to allow them to man lesser weapons when the need arose, and thus, on the first day of the invasion, Company A of the 83rd Battalion produced a bazooka team which knocked out an enemy tank during a counter-attack. The following day mortar fire was used to engage a group of Italian tanks; while none was hit directly, the fire was intense enough to cause them to start up and move, and the mortar shells 'sheep-dogged' them along until they were in a position to be reached by artillery and effectively put out of action. On another occasion a disabled German tank was still active enough with its gun to make life difficult for some US infantry; they asked if the mortar battalion could help, and by way of an answer the mortars fired eight rounds. The tank was silenced immediately; subsequent examination showed that seven shells had landed within 15yd of the tank while the eighth had dropped straight into the open turret hatch and burst inside the tank.

As a result of these and similar activities, the 4.2in was accepted as a worthwhile weapon, and from then on was in continual demand in every theatre. As might be expected, the Sicilian campaign showed one or two minor shortcomings in organization and handling, but these were soon corrected. As far as the weapon itself was concerned, the only observation was the usual one – please can we have some more range? Originally the mortar could propel the high-explosive shell to 2,400yd (2,200m); this was improved to 3,200yd (2,903m) in January 1943 by the adoption of a new propelling charge, and in March 1943 another improvement in the propellant chemistry allowed 4,500yd (4,115m) to be reached. But in spite of this range being reached in trials, the CWS felt that adoption of it would automatically lead to people using it at maximum range all the time, and it was not felt that the weapon could stand up to prolonged full-charge firing; consequently the official maximum range was retained at 3,200yd. Much argument arose over this decision, and as reports from various theatres seemed to justify the demands for full range, the restriction was rescinded and the 4,500yd figure became the official range.

Marine Mortars

In the South Pacific, the first use of the 4.2in was in September 1943 on Guadalcanal. This was followed by action on Bougainville, where the mortars were found to be invaluable in jungle conditions where the usual 105mm and 155mm howitzers could not cope. One of the most interesting mortar manifestations in the Pacific theatre was the mounting of mortars in landing craft to form 'mortar boats'. The idea had been tentatively suggested for the Sicily landings, but not proceeded with in that action. It was then broached by the CWS in Oahu, and the US Navy began making some tests. Eventually the navy developed a method of mounting mortars into Landing Craft Tank, and early in 1944 produced three craft with mortars for use in the invasion of Saipan. Unfortunately, these were lashed to the deck of a landing ship to make the trip to the scene of the landings, and during a storm en route two were washed overboard. The third was destroyed in Pearl Harbor when the carrying ship suddenly exploded. After this disheartening beginning the project was modified and called for

the use of three mortars in a Landing Craft Infantry, all firing forward over the bows, and with the forward troop compartments converted into magazines to carry 3,600 shells. These boats were finally used in the invasion of the Palau Islands on 15 September 1944, supporting the landings of the 1st Marine Division. Firing while cruising slowly offshore, or firing from anchored positions, the mortars proved to be highly effective in providing covering fire for the marine assault, and in subsequent days they were frequently called upon to deliver retaliatory fire, barrages and on-call fire to help marine units on shore. In spite of their floating gun positions, the fire was remarkably accurate.

Experimental Enlargements

This sort of activity soon proved the worth of well-handled mortars, and the inevitable result followed. Just as in the World War I the question now heard was, if a 4.2in is good, how much better would a bigger one be? After one or two tentative design studies, work began on producing a 105mm mortar, little more than an improved 4.2in in general appearance. Firing a 35lb (16kg) bomb to 4,000yd (3,660m) it was successful, but there was so little improvement over the 4.2in that production would hardly have been worthwhile. If there had to be a new mortar, it was felt, then it might as well be a significant improvement. And so the 155mm T36 model was born.

This was still a conventional smooth-bored weapon, but which used a shock-absorbing system between bipod and barrel as did the Soviet models. A limited number were manufactured late in 1944 and sent to the South West Pacific for evaluation in combat. Firing a 60lb finned bomb to 2,200yd (2,010m) it made very satisfactory noises at the target end and had quite good accuracy. But the range was insufficient for the effort expended in emplacing and firing the weapon and, while it had its uses in the somewhat specialized conditions in the South West Pacific Theatre, it was not retained after the war ended.

Meanwhile, even heavier models were being considered. First, the 240mm T35, a breech-loading, rifled mortar firing a 250lb (113kg) shell at 1,000ft (304m) per second to over 9,000 yards (8,200m). Then a 250mm smooth-bore firing a 250lb bomb to 7,500yd (6,860m); this had originally been a 10in model early in 1945, and was rechristened 250mm and earmarked for peacetime development but, like all the other mortar projects, was abandoned early in 1946.

Mobile Mortars

The outstanding contribution of the United States to the war, in the eyes of many people, was its undoubted efficiency in designing and producing automotive equipment. From jeeps to bulldozers, graders, shovels, deuce-and-a-half trucks, tank transporters and scooters, the production of the US automobile industry put the Allies on wheels or tracks all over the globe, and the number of schemes evolved in the USA for putting some of those wheels or tracks underneath some sort of weapon were legion. Self-propelled guns and howitzers were designed, scrapped, redesigned, adopted and used in a wide variety of types, and it can hardly be surprising to find that the prospect of producing self-propelled mortars was not overlooked.

The first ideas were largely to try to overcome the problem of moving a mortar about in the front line without exposing the overburdened squad to enemy fire. These ideas seem to have come to a head early in 1944 and from then on a number of possible systems made their appearance. The 81mm mortar was mounted in the bed of a half-track, along with a .50 calibre machine gun, to make the mortar carrier M21; the mortar carrier M4A1 was the same thing without the machine gun. Then came the T27 and T29, projects to mount the 81mm mortar in a turretless tracked vehicle derived from a redundant M5A3 light tank chassis, but this was thought to be too much chassis for too little firepower and the project was closed. The 4.2in also found its way into a half-track as the T21 and into the M24 light tank chassis as the T64, but these too came to nothing.

The 155mm mortar T36 was placed in a rebuilt M4 tank, the turret being re-designed to take a ball mounting which allowed the mortar to reach 60 degrees of elevation. Proposed in February 1945, this looked so promising that it was authorized to be continued as a peacetime project, one pilot model to be built for testing and evaluation, but it never got past the mock-up stage, the project being terminated in December 1945.

In the hopes of getting something into action quickly, the 155mm motor mortar carrier T96 was proposed, mounting the mortar in the open body of the M37 105mm howitzer carriage, but this too

One of several half-track designs, the US Army's M21 mortar carrier had the 81mm mortar firing to the front of the vehicle.

was overtaken by the end of the war and quietly axed. Abortive as these projects were, they form an interesting backdrop to the subsequent post-war development of mobile mortar carriers.

Little David

To complete the story of American mortars in World War II we need to look at Little David. During the war years every army had some form of homemade large-calibre mortar as a device for testing aerial bombs. Suppose you have developed a concrete-piercing bomb. To prove that it works you have to drop it and penetrate a slab of concrete. But dropping it from 20,000ft or so, as would happen in real life, means there is more than a good chance you are going to miss your 6ft square test slab of concrete. So you calculate what its striking velocity would be if dropped from the appropriate height. Then you design a mortar and calculate what charge you need to launch the bomb out of this mortar so that it lands a couple of hundred yards away at the correct striking velocity. Then you build a mortar and test your bomb.

The US Army Air Force had a 'bomb testing device T1', and early in 1944, when plans were being laid for Operation *Olympic*, the invasion of the Japanese mainland, it occurred to somebody

that in view of the various fortifications that might be encountered, some powerful demolition weapon would be an advantage. The bomb testing device would furnish the barrel; all that was needed was some sort of mounting and a suitable projectile. The mortar was a rifled muzzle-loader with the elevating arc attached to the breech end. For transportation, it was lifted from its mounting and towed behind an M26 tank transporter tractor, the elevating arc being attached to the tractor and the muzzle riding on an eight-wheeled trolley.

The mounting was nothing more than a steel box, 18ft long, 11ft wide and 10ft deep, sunk into a pit. Inside this box was the elevating gear, traversing gear, and six hydraulic jacks which were used for mounting and dismounting the barrel. The box was towed by another M26 tractor, being fitted with wheels for travelling. On arrival on site, the pit was carved out by a bulldozer and the box was winched down a ramp. Its wheels were then removed and the excavated earth was pushed back and packed around the box walls as a support. The barrel was then towed across the top on a steel runway and lifted by the jacks from its trolley and lowered into place.

The whole performance of assembly took about 12 hours. Loading was done by a special crane; the charge was inserted into the muzzle and rammed into the chamber. The shell was then

Little David on the march; the barrel assembly being towed by a tank transporter tractor.

The barrel of Little David as it is today in Aberdeen Proving Ground. The trunnion bearings and elevation rack are well displayed here. The end of the mounting box can be seen at the left edge.

Another picture at Aberdeen, showing the shell for Little David.

presented to the muzzle and the pre-engraved driving band was engaged in the rifling. The shell was rammed into the bore for a few inches and the mortar was then elevated so that the loading was completed by gravity.

The shell was a peculiar shape, with a long conical nose and a hemispherical base. It weighed 3,700lb (1,680kg) and was loaded with 1,600lb (725kg) of Picratol high explosive. The whole weapon weighed about 81 tons (8,230kg) when in position and could fire its shell to a range of 9,500yd (8,690m).

By the middle of 1945 the design was finalized and being tested. Operation *Olympic* was scheduled for November and it was agreed that it would have its service acceptance test in September so that it could be shipped across the Pacific in good time. But the Army Service Force expressed itself dissatisfied with the accuracy tests and insisted on postponing the acceptance

A wartime picture showing the whole '914mm mortar' in position.

The German 10cm Nebelwerfer 40 was closer to being a howitzer than it was to being a mortar; due to its complexity and expense, relatively few were manufactured.

until the ballistics had been further investigated. Then came the atomic bomb, and *Olympic* promptly dissolved. In October 1945 Little David was sent to Aberdeen Proving Ground and that is where it has remained ever since, as part of the outdoor museum.

SOME GERMAN IMPROVEMENTS

In the German Army the mortar was widely and effectively employed, though since the standard designs appeared to satisfy the army there was little attempt to improve performance. The 5cm Granatwerfer 36 was less and less used as the war became one of movement, and by 1942 it was

virtually obsolescent. It was generally replaced with a shortened version of the 81mm, the Short Model 42, popularly called the Stummelwerfer (stumpy mortar). This fired the same bombs as the standard weapon to 2,000m (1,200yd), weighed only 28kg (62lb) complete, and became a particular favourite with airborne and SS troops. The Nebeltruppen had their 10cm weapon replaced by a newer version, the 10cm NbW 40, with a wheeled carriage. Much heavier and more robust than its predecessor – 775kg as opposed to 105kg – this increase was justified by its increased performance, the range going up from 3,020m (3,300yd) to 6,220m (6,800yd), but not many of these were issued, since the Nebeltruppen were soon issued with their distinctive six-barrel rocket launchers and these eventually replaced all mortars in Nebeltruppen service.

The best German mortar of the war was, in

fact, not German; it was Russian. As already mentioned, the Soviets had developed a very good 120mm mortar in 1938. Firing a 15kg (34lb) bomb to 5,700m (6,235yd) and weighing only 272kg (600lb) in firing order, it was an ingenious design with a lightweight two-wheeled carriage. It could be dropped into action very rapidly and the range and size of bomb made it a very unwelcome addition to the battlefield as far as the Germans were concerned; indeed, it is probably fair to say that it was the best mortar of the war. The German Army was so impressed with its performance and mobility that after capturing a few and making some trials, it was forthwith put into production as the Granatwerfer 42. Once sufficient numbers were available it became the preferred mortar throughout the army, largely replacing all the other types, and even infantry gun companies were re-equipped with them.

The oddest German mortar was the 20cm Leichte Ladungswerfer – light charge thrower. This was a lightweight mortar with a heavyweight punch; it was a simple 9mm spigot, mounted on a baseplate and supported by the usual form of bipod and traversing gear. The end of the spigot was formed into a bayonet-type catch, and into this snapped a special cartridge. Then a 22kg (49lb) finned bomb was loaded by slipping its hollow tail unit over the cartridge and spigot. The cartridge was fired electrically, blowing the bomb off the spigot to a maximum range of about 685m (750yd). This may not sound much, but the bomb was surprisingly accurate, and it carried a charge of 7kg (15lb) of TNT with a delayed-action fuze. Its prime function was to deal with obstinate small strongpoints, and there is no doubt that the delivery of such a bomb onto the roof of a small pillbox or reinforced house would rapidly convince the occupants of the folly of their enterprise.

AND SOME RUSSIAN GIANTS

In Russia, the success of the 120mm mortar rebounded to some extent when the Germans copied it, but this caused little dismay. The mortar had peculiar advantages for the Soviet Army: it was simple to operate, hence the gunners needed little training; it was cheap to make, hence factories could produce them in large numbers; the ammunition was relatively simple, so the

A Finnish 160mm mortar based upon the Soviet wartime design; it may look like just another mortar but that barrel is almost ten feet long.

same thing applied there; and after all was said and done it was an efficient man-killing tool. These considerations pointed to it being just the thing the Soviets needed to arm their rapidly expanding armies after the initial setbacks, and more and more mortars began to flow from the factories. But as well as using them in the accepted infantry role, the Soviets went one step further and began to produce really heavy mortars and equip artillery units with them, After the 120mm came a 160mm and then a 240mm, powerful weapons on wheeled mountings which could reach as far as many artillery howitzers and do a lot more damage with their heavy bombs and high rate of fire. The 160mm could send an 40kg (88lb) bomb to 7,315m (8,000yd) and keep up a rate of fire of three rounds a minute, while the 240mm fired a 136kg (300lb) bomb every thirty seconds to 10,980m (12,000yd). Regiments of these weapons were produced and became an integral part of the 'Artillery Armies' which were to sweep the German invasion out of Russia and back to Berlin in 1945.

As might be imagined, muzzle-loading a 40kg bomb into a 160mm mortar was out of the question, and thus a breech-loading mortar was developed. The mortar consisted of a fairly normal baseplate and tripod, but the two were connected by a simple trough with a set of trunnion bearings at its top end. The barrel, with trunnions fitting into these bearings, lay in the trough for firing, and the trough and barrel were elevated by the usual gears in the front tripod. To load, however, the barrel was unlocked from the trough and the breech end swung upwards, the barrel turning about the trunnions, until the barrel was more or less horizontal. The simple breech was then opened, a conventional finned bomb loaded, the breech closed and the barrel pushed back down into the trough and locked. The firing lanyard was then pulled to trip the firing pin and fire the bomb. The rate of fire was not particularly fast, but certainly faster than a conventional howitzer of the same calibre would have been. Both the 160mm and 240mm were built with this sort of breech mechanism and both were to survive for a very long time after the Second World War.

5 The Accurate Mortar

After the end of World War II, mortar development came to a standstill. The weapons which had served so well in the war were retained for future use, but what money and design facilities that still existed were usually committed to more spectacular researches – such as rockets and missiles. The Korean War was fought with the mortars which had seen the end of World War II, the British using their 3in and 4.2in, the US Army its 81mm and 4.2in, and the North Koreans and Chinese People's Volunteers a scratch collection of ex-Japanese and ex-Soviet weapons. Their principal model appeared to be the Soviet 8lmm, which gives a chance to tell my favourite mortar story.

The scene is a hilltop in Korea, late in 1951. The Communist troops had just been dispossessed of a piece of real estate and the British infantry were digging in to prepare for the inevitable counter-attack; I was part of the artillery forward observer's party. All over the hilltop small groups of men were digging slit trenches, and amid them stalked their Regimental Sergeant Major, impeccably dressed, stick beneath his arm, watching his men dig – and listening. Soon came the telltale ripple of explosions from the north which announced the firing of mortars; the RSM continued his unhurried pacing, counting mentally. At the appropriate moment, with a voice which could have been heard from Pyongyang to Pusan, he roared 'Get down!' and every man on the hill – except the RSM – hit the dirt. Down came the bombs, loud explosions, smoke and splinters, eruptions of dirt. When it all cleared the RSM was still standing there, to bellow 'Get up! Go on digging!' And every man got up, seized his pick or shovel, and delved deeper into Korea. He kept this up for over half an hour until the position was to his satisfaction; he must have had a charmed life.

COUNTERING THE MORTAR

In the 1950s more interest began to be taken in the mortar, as well as a good deal of interest in the question of how best to counter-attack it. It seems a well-established fact that every combatant of World War II has a tendency to underplay his own mortars, while speaking with some feeling about the effect of his enemy's mortar fire, and in the 1950s this fact seemed to come to the forefront. During these years there was an immense amount of research into the application of electronics to military matters and the whole picture is a tangled thicket of interrelated projects and spin-offs, so that it takes a superhuman detective to trace many of the projects to their source, even if the information was available. For various reasons the information is not readily available, but it seems very likely that the first step along the trail of the counter-mortar was, in fact, counter-artillery. After some success in developing radar-computer systems to track missiles, both the USA and the UK began to look into the possibility of developing some sort of radar to track artillery shells in flight, deduce their trajectory in some way, and then extrapolate back along the trajectory to find the weapon which had fired the shell. One could then supply this information to a gun battery and open counter-fire on the enemy weapon with speed and accuracy. While this sounds very attractive, the trouble is that most modern weapons of the gun-howitzer class, such as the US and British 105mm field weapons, have multiple charge systems and a variety of projectiles of differing ballistic performance, plus a range of elevation from something like −5 degrees to +70 degrees. This all means that there is a multiplicity of trajectory paths which a shell could describe to land at the same spot, and trying to programme a computer to sort out the options and come up with a sensible answer was almost impossible at that time. However, in the course of examining the problem, it occurred to the designers that the average mortar tends to fire on a fairly constant sort of trajectory, and if it could be tracked in the sky and plotted, there was a good chance that this problem could be solved.

In fact, of course, it had been done during the war in a somewhat more primitive fashion. In 1943 the British had begun using a gun-laying radar (as used with anti-aircraft guns) to track weather balloons and provide more accurate data than could be achieved by optical instruments. It was suggested that it might be possible to detect mortar bombs in flight, but experiments were not encouraging and the idea was dropped – partly because it smacked too much of the defensive, and at that time the higher command desired everybody to think offensively. But once the invasion force had landed in 1944 and had become acquainted with the German mortars – and each German infantry division had fifty-seven 81mm and twelve 120mm mortars by that time – the experiments were revived. This time the results were better – people were learning more about radar every day in the early 1940s – and a primitive system of spotting two or three successive bombs in the early part of the trajectory was developed, from which with pencil and paper a trajectory could be deduced and which was sometimes quite close to the truth. But then, in late 1944, the auto-tracking Radar No. 3 Mark 7 appeared, and this transformed the location of bombs almost overnight. The radar scanned an area and picked up a bomb on the upward leg of its trajectory. The operator locked on and stopped his bearing and range dials,

locating the bomb in space. He allowed the radar to track for a brief interval and then locked a second set of dials, producing a second fix. From these two it was relatively easy to plot back and locate the mortar to within 50yd or even 25yd. However, acquiring the radars, converting them by the addition of extra dials and circuitry, and training operators all took time, and radar location of mortars was still in its experimental days when the war ended. And with the general winding-down after the war it stayed that way for some years; the technique was kept in being, but no counter-mortar radar units were formed.

THE MORTAR RENAISSANCE

In the late 1950s the mortar suddenly became an object of interest. A number of unfortunate accidents with mortars in Korea, when the intense cold led to tail fins shattering on firing and causing the bombs to fall short, had shown that the old 'cheap and cheerful' ideas of design had to be radically changed. In 1957 the Royal Armaments Research & Design Establishment (RARDE), at Fort Halstead, Kent, set about developing an 81mm mortar to replace the 3in.

The weak link in mortar design was the vexed question of windage, which is the difference between the inside diameter of the barrel and the outside diameter of the bomb. Too little, and the bomb trapped the air behind it and took an age to slide down the bore and failed to land hard enough to set off the cap in the primary cartridge. Too much, and the bomb was literally bouncing off the sides of the tube on the way up; high-speed photography showed that bombs came out of the muzzle at such an angle that for the first few hundred feet of flight they were yawing up to 50 or 60 degrees off the theoretical trajectory, and what that did to the accuracy can be imagined. Another defect was that the fins of the bomb were almost always too close to the body; unless you resorted to hinged fins which opened like a penknife, the fins had to be of the same calibre as the bomb, and if these were too close to the body they lived in a thin-air region, if not a near-vacuum, as the bomb went through the air and the airstream swept back outside the fins. Only by putting the fins well behind the major diameter of the bomb could you expect them to have any effect on stabilizing the flight. The average bomb, too, was no bargain from the aerodynamic point of view, with its blunt nose and tapering tail or, even worse, blunt nose, cylindrical body and blunt tail. And, of course, all these things had their roots in the original 'keep it cheap and simple' doctrine which had dominated mortar design since 1915.

Designing a mortar, with constraints of cost loosened, was relatively easy – high-grade steel for the barrel, strong alloys for the baseplate, the

best elevation and traverse controls and sights that experience could provide, and the design practically dictated itself. The most complex and difficult part was redesigning the bomb, and what RARDE produced was revolutionary. The bomb body was no longer tear-drop shaped but almost elliptical, with a long tapering nose and an equally long and smoothly tapering tail. Behind this came a machined light alloy tail boom and fins, all in one piece, of such dimensions that the fins were well back and in the converging air stream as it swept over the bomb. The ultimate refinement lay in the method of sealing the escape of gas around the bomb and of controlling the windage. There was the usual carefully machined bourrelet around the waist of the bomb (and the tips of the fins were equally carefully machined to

Coldstream Guardsmen firing an 81mm mortar during exercises in Germany in 1978.

This picture of the 81mm mortar shows the construction of the bipod and traversing head and also shows the result of prolonged firing in soft ground: the baseplate digs itself deeper with every shot.

a diameter very slightly less than that of the interior of the barrel) and into this machined surface a groove was cut. And into the groove went a carefully shaped sealing ring of heat-resistant Makrolon plastic material which acted as a skirt. In its normal state it lay flush with the bourrelet of the bomb, so that there was sufficient windage for the bomb to slide down the barrel at a good speed. On striking the firing pin and firing the propelling charge, the rush of gas up the side of the bomb forced this 'skirt' outwards against the bore, while the inner end was forced tightly into the machined seat of the groove. The result was an almost perfect gas-tight seal around the bomb, which also by virtue of its design centred the bomb perfectly in the bore so that there was negligible chance of yaw as it left the muzzle.

In one bound the mortar had gone from being an area weapon to being very nearly a point-target weapon; with the 3in mortar you could generally guarantee getting the bomb into a football field, but with the 81mm RARDE mortar you could choose into which penalty area to drop the bomb. The 3in had fired a 10lb (4.5kg) bomb to a maximum range of 2,600yd (2,380m); the 81mm fired a 9lb 6oz (4.3kg) bomb to 5,650yd (5,170m); And because the bomb was of a higher quality metal (spheroidal graphited cast iron), specially designed to produce the maximum number of optimum-sized fragments and filled with RDX/TNT, its target effect was greatly increased.

The 81mm mortar L16 began entering service in 1961. There were a few modifications before the design settled down; the baseplate was replaced by a fresh design produced by the Canadian Armaments Research Department, the original propelling charge was simplified and improved, and a new sight, also of Canadian origin, was adopted. The range of ammunition was extended to include illuminating and smoke bombs, and after a good deal of testing and discussion, the US Army adopted the British design as its 81mm Mortar M252 in 1974, initially purchasing some 400 from Britain, after which more were licence-built in the USA.

The Americans had also been quick to copy the British design of bomb for their earlier 81mm M29 mortar, but they later developed a refinement of their own by slightly canting the fins so as to impart a slow spin to the bomb which, they claim, increases the accuracy. Other nations soon followed, and by the mid-1980s the British 81mm bomb design had been copied all over the world and in a variety of calibres.

THE RISE OF THE HEAVY MORTAR

The other post-war mortar surprise was the rise and rise of the 120mm mortar. As we have seen, this was due to the Russian mortar being copied by the German Army and used with very good effect by them. Like other wartime designs, it

UK 81mm

Ordnance, ML, 81mm, L16A1

Calibre	81.4mm (3.2in)
Barrel length	1,280mm (50in)
Weight in action	37.85kg (83lb)
Elevation	800 to 1,422mils (+40 degrees to +80 degrees)
Weight of bomb	4.2kg (9.2lb)
Muzzle velocity	297m/sec (975ft/sec)
Minimum range	180m (197yd)
Maximum range	5,650m (6,180yd)

This was really the father of modern mortar design, particularly in relation to its ammunition, and it took the mortar out of the 'area weapon' category and gave it accuracy and consistency which had rarely been seen before.

The construction of the weapon is quite conventional, with a barrel, baseplate and bipod. The barrel is ribbed over the chamber and for about half its length in order to dissipate heat; it is heavier than originally specified so that it can be used with any 81mm ammunition employed by any NATO army and it can maintain a steady rate of 15 rounds per minute indefinitely without overheating. The rear end is closed by a separate breech plug which contains the firing pin and is screwed into the barrel. This plug terminates on a ball unit which fits into the socket in the baseplate.

The baseplate is circular and deeply webbed on the under-surface. It is of forged aluminium and gives good support in most conditions, though additional flotation is required on boggy ground.

The bipod is of a rather unusual shape, designed so that the elevating screw moves within one of the legs and thus saves weight by not requiring a separate casing. There is a short traversing screw at the top of the elevating rod which permits 100mils (approximately 5.5 degrees) of traverse each side of centre at 800mils (45 degrees) elevation.

The sight is an optical panoramic sight that can also be used with the general purpose machine gun.

Ammunition provided for the 81mm mortar includes HE, smoke and illuminating rounds; the propelling charge consists of a primary cartridge and six secondary cartridges which fit around the tail boom.

The 81mm L16 has been adopted by the USA as its M252 mortar; it has also been manufactured under licence in Japan by the Howa Machinery Company and is used by the Japanese Self-Defense Force. Other countries employing this mortar include Austria, Brazil, Canada, India, Norway and Portugal.

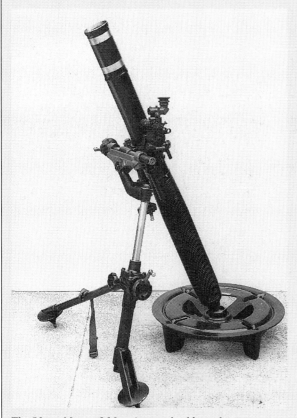

The 81mm Mortar L16 on its standard baseplate.

Setting the sight on the 81mm mortar. The liability of the baseplate to be driven into soft ground is common to every mortar.

The white phosphorus smoke bomb for the 81mm mortar, together with more bombs in their transit packages.

Soldiers of the Royal Regiment of Wales firing the 81mm mortar during a training exercise in Germany shortly after its introduction.

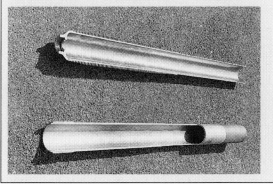

The barrel of the 81mm mortar (left) compared to the barrel of its predecessor, the 3in mortar. The modern design is thinner and lighter yet stronger, and is liberally provided with cooling fins.

The American M29A1 mortar replaced the wartime 81mm M1 and had the barrel finned for its full length and a recoil-absorber mounted above the barrel. It was replaced in service by the M252, the US version of the British L16 mortar.

The Danish 120mm M50 mortar was one of many licensed versions of the first Hotchkiss-Brandt post-war design. A robust weapon with a recoil-absorber between the barrel and the bipod, it had a maximum range of about 6,500m (7,000yd).

could obviously stand some improvement, and the French Hotchkiss-Brandt company, the successors of Edgar Brandt, set about overhauling their pre-war model. They produced a fairly conventional design which did not really improve all that much on the wartime models, but then they threw caution to the winds and came up with a 120mm rifled weapon which opened several eyes and just about put paid to any idea of lightweight infantry-supporting artillery.

The Brandt 120mm Mortier Rayée was unusual in that it fired off its wheels. It had the usual sort of barrel, albeit rifled, attached to the usual sort of baseplate. But instead of a bipod or tripod to support the barrel, there was a short elevating and traversing standard, the lower end of which was attached to an axle that had a wheel at each end. In action the wheels were locked and the barrel elevated and traversed above it. To go out of action, the wheels were unlocked and run back towards the barrel until the barrel could be locked into a clamp on the axle. The muzzle was then pulled down, using the wheels and axle as a fulcrum, thus lifting the baseplate out of the ground. A muzzle cap with a towing eye was attached, and the whole thing hooked on behind the towing vehicle. Going into action was the reverse: unhook, let the muzzle go up, dropping

The Danish 120mm M50 packed for travelling.

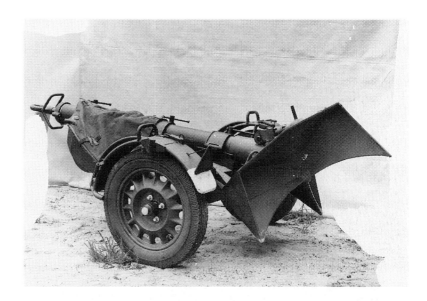

The Hotchkiss-Brandt 120mm rifled mortar can be towed behind virtually any light vehicle.

the baseplate, unclamp the barrel, run the wheels forward and lock them.

Brandt approached the rifling question from a different direction to the American system. The bomb was an odd shape, a cross between an artillery shell and a mortar bomb, with a long tapering nose and then a parallel-sided section with an artillery-style driving band, then a short taper to a reduced-diameter base, and a propellant container screwed into it rather like a conventional mortar bomb tail unit with the fins removed. The problem of drop-loading a rifled mortar was solved by pre-engraving the driving band with the necessary grooves to fit the rifling and then putting a plastic obturating (sealing) ring behind the driving band. The loader has to be careful to fit the driving band

The 120mm rifled mortar in the firing position.

The 120mm Hotchkiss-Brandt rifled mortar in the early throes of electronic fire control. The master computer is on the hood of the truck, while the gun commander is operating a hand-held computer for calculating corrections.

into the grooves of the barrel rifling, after which he lets the bomb go as usual. When it reaches the bottom of the tube the firing pin strikes the cap and the propelling charge explodes in the usual way. The rush of gas hits the plastic obturating band and forces it into the rifling, so sealing all the pressure behind the bomb; and the bomb is then driven out of the tube by the gas, with the driving band engaging the grooves in the rifling and thus giving the bomb the desired spin. There is a small delay element in the front end of the cartridge container tube, and this burns through and fires a tiny charge which blows the tube off the bomb during the first part of the trajectory, so that the tube lands about 100yd away from the muzzle. The conventional type of bomb fired from a smooth-bore mortar weighed 13kg (29lb) and ranged to 5,000m (5,470yd); the rifled bomb weighed 18kg (40lb) and went to 8,350m (9,135yd).

Considering that this mortar weighed about 580kg (1,280lb) and could be towed behind virtually any light vehicle, this was quite a remarkable performance. But the Thompson-Brandt company was not satisfied, and sat down to consider how to extend the range of the mortar without adding weight or exceeding the safety limits.

Rocket Technology

The solution chosen was rocket assistance. The bomb was, externally, just the same as already described, with a pre-engraved driving band and a tail tube carrying the propelling charge. But inside the bomb, centrally placed and well insulated from the surrounding high-explosive charge, was a rocket motor terminating in a venturi nozzle in the base of the bomb. This was plugged, after which the tail tube was fitted. On firing, the bomb left the mortar and the tail tube blew off and fell away, just as with the standard bomb. But in this case as the tail tube blew itself off it also ignited a ten-second delay unit inside the rocket nozzle plug. At the end of ten seconds, while the bomb was still on the upwards leg of its flight, the delay burned through and ignited the rocket motor which, of course, blew the plug out of the nozzle. The rocket then accelerated the bomb, lifting its trajectory height and thus extending the range. From 8,350m, the maximum range was increased to 13,000m (14,220yd); the only downside to the design was the loss of a small portion of the high-explosive bursting charge, but the bomb still had a powerful effect at the target.

Having done the trick with the rifled mortar, Thomson-Brandt then turned to the conventional smooth-bore, fin-stabilized mortar and set about designing a rocket-assisted bomb for that. This was a little more difficult – on the standard bomb the fins were on the end of the tail tube, and, obviously, if you blew this off in order to give the rocket free play, then you blew off your stabilizing system and the bomb could go anywhere. The answer to this dilemma was to move the fins up and put them on the rear end of the bomb body, retaining the tail tube solely as a means of carrying the propelling charge, just as in the rifled bomb. However, as noted earlier, if calibre-sized fins are put too close to the body the air goes over them and they have little or no effect. So the designers made the fins well over-calibre and hinged them so that they folded close to the body and were under-calibre when loading. On firing, the bomb was blown out of the barrel in the normal way and within a very short space the tail tube was blown off. In doing so it unlocked the fins which then swung out to their full diameter and began their stabilizing function. At the same time, the ten-second delay was ignited and at the end of its burning time it fired the rocket motor. The conventional bomb for the smooth-bore 120mm mortar weighed 13kg (29lb) and could go up to 7,000m (7660yd), depending upon which model of mortar was used; the first rocket-assisted bomb weighed 20kg and went to 6,550m (7,165yd), not exactly what was hoped for. A redesign, producing a lighter (13.4kg) bomb, produced a maximum range of 8,950 metres, and this was thought to be satisfactory.

COUNTERING THE MORTAR, PHASE TWO

The invention of the transistor in the mid-1950s propelled electronics into an entirely new phase of development and, indirectly perhaps, led to an upsurge in computer technology. It became

'Green Archer' was the first British purpose-built mortar-locating radar. This picture, taken in the early 1960s, shows one of the first models, with the antenna folded down over the transmitter unit.

possible to make computers tailored to specific tasks, more compact than before and using less power. It also allowed radars and other electronic apparatus to be made more robust and more reliable. And before long, the question of locating mortars by radar came under review once more.

The system that finally evolved is much the same whoever makes radar; a scanning antenna picks up a bomb on the early part of its trajectory, fixes it in space and stores the fix in an electronic memory; the antenna then moves up quickly (usually by beam-switching rather than physically moving the antenna structure) so as to catch the same bomb a second time, still on the upward part of its flight, stores this second fix, and also stores the time elapsed between the fixes.

The two fixes, the time interval and the position of the radar are now fed into a computer which reconstructs the trajectory between the two points, then extends this back until it hits the ground, so deducing the mortar's position. There are, obviously, some refinements. For example, the relative heights of mortar and radar have an effect on the computation, and suitable 'fiddle factors' have to be introduced to deal with this, but that, in a nutshell, is how a counter-mortar radar works and it works very well. Before the bomb has landed, the co-ordinates of the mortar

are in the hands of an artillery battery who can then fire before the mortar manages to get many more bombs off, and as a result mortar firing as a pastime quickly loses its charm. It is a poor counter-mortar radar that cannot produce a fix to within 25m, and that is close enough to make life unpleasant when a 155mm shell arrives.

One might therefore suppose that the general adoption of counter-mortar radar would have led to the gradual disappearance of the mortar; but in fact nothing of the sort happened. If anything, the use of mortars has increased, with the US and Canadian armies, for example, which never used heavy mortars before, both adopting 120mm models in the 1980s. The reason is partly a matter of calculating the risk: mortar-locating radars are expensive devices and, in peacetime, tend to be at the bottom of the shopping list for all but the most affluent of armies. The odds, therefore, are still with the mortar; in a brush-fire war the chances of a mortar coming up against a locating radar are negligible and the risk is worth taking. It is also partly a matter of calculating the economic benefits: mortars, even the most involved designs, are cheaper than conventional tube artillery, their ammunition is also less expensive, their operation is rather simpler and they require less of an infrastructure to support them. And, reverting

'Cymbeline' replaced 'Green Archer' in the 1970s; it does the same job but with more advanced computing technology it can deal with a wider range of projectiles.

US 120mm

120mm Battalion Mortar M120/M121

Calibre	120mm (4.7in)
Barrel length	1.758m (69.2in)
Weight in action	145kg (320lb)
Elevation	+40 degrees to +85 degrees
Weight of bomb	13.2kg (29.1lb)
Muzzle velocity	102 to 320m/sec (335 to 1,050ft/sec)
Minimum range	170m (186yd)
Maximum range	7,240m (921yd)

In the mid-1980s the US Army decided that the 107mm mortar (which had started life as the 4.2in in the 1920s) was no longer a viable weapon on today's battlefield, and it began examining the various 120mm mortars then on offer. In 1990 the army settled on the Soltam K6 light model, developed in Israel from a Finnish original design, and they adopted it in two forms, the M120 in the normal towed infantry form, and the M121 when mounted into an armoured personnel carrier. The original demand was for almost 2,100 mortars, but this was later reduced to 1,725, sufficient to replace the existing 107mm weapons, and the major proportion of these were M121 versions to be mounted into modified M113 APCs.

The M120 is a quite conventional 120mm weapon, with circular baseplate, alloy steel smooth-bore barrel and bipod with the usual range of adjustment and with twin shock absorbers connecting it to the barrel. The prime aim in this particular design was to obtain a powerful mortar but at a level of weight which would allow it to be carried by men in an emergency or towed behind the lightest of vehicles, or pack-loaded on mules. The mortar is provided with a lightweight trailer upon which the complete mortar can be loaded without requiring it to be dismantled. It also carries six rounds of ammunition for emergency use, plus the requisite tools, sights and cleaning equipment.

Work is currently in progress to develop a ceramic barrel which would retain the same strength but be a great deal lighter. Much work is also being done on developing an entirely new range of ammunition, including a long-range bomb to reach to 10,000m (10,950yd), a carrier bomb loaded with small anti-personnel mines, a guided anti-tank bomb and an anti-personnel bomb loaded with flechettes.

The M120 mortar in the firing position, with its transporting trailer in the background.

US 120mm *continued*

Above: *The M120 mortar packed and ready to move.*

Left: *The M121 mortar on its turntable baseplate for assembly into the M1064 carrier, a modification of the M113 APC.*

once more to the mortar-locating radar threat, the light 'grenade thrower' type of mortar has become more efficient but is still using a small bomb with a relatively low trajectory height, which can easily be missed by auto-hunting radars primed to look higher up for bigger bombs.

The British Army decided to replace its 2in mortar in the 1970s and, no doubt hoping for a second tour de force like the 81mm L16, RARDE duly produced a 51mm model which set out to be everything it was believed that the infantryman would require. One feature was the ability to fire at extremely short ranges so as to cover the zone usually thought to be the area in which rifle grenades held sway, but to cover it with a high-trajectory weapon which could get behind walls and into ditches that the conventional low-trajectory rifle grenade could not reach. This endeavour, praiseworthy as it was, fell down in practice. The mortar was a quite normal design

but had, as an accessory, a spacer containing an auxiliary firing pin. This was dropped into the barrel and took up several inches of space, so that when the bomb was dropped it came to rest about two-thirds of the way down the barrel and was fired by the auxiliary firing pin, which was in turn impelled by the regular firing pin's action. All very similar in principle, if not in actual design, to the Japanese 'knee mortar'. But to attain the shortest ranges only the primary cartridge was used, and the amount of gas involved was not really sufficient to fill the void behind the bomb while also generating a reasonable propulsive force. The bombs sometimes failed to leave the mortar, and when they did leave, their flight was somewhat erratic. A short period of experience soon convinced the users that they did not really need this accessory and the idea was abandoned. The charge system was redesigned so that the normal propelling charge could be reduced to

Loading and firing the 51mm mortar can be done as a one-man task, though two men make it easier.

UK 51mm

Ordnance ML 51mm Mortar L9A1

Calibre	51mm (1.99in)
Barrel length	750mm (29.25in)
Weight in action	5.65kg (12.46lb)
Elevation	800–1600mils (45 degrees – 90 degrees)
Weight of bomb	920g (32.5oz)
Muzzle velocity	103m/sec (338ft/sec)
Minimum range	50m (55yd)
Maximum range	800m (875yd)

Development of this mortar, as a replacement for the 1930s 2in model, began in the early 1970s at the RARDE at Fort Halstead, Kent. In its original form it was provided with a monopod leg and with a special 'short range insert' which could be dropped into the barrel so as to enlarge the chamber space and thus reduce the velocity and range to a minimum of 50m (55yd).

The mortar, without the monopod, was introduced in 1982 as a conventional hand-held weapon with a small curved support spade beneath the breech. The firing mechanism was of the self-cocking type, operated by a lever. The short-range insert carried a supplementary firing pin which was driven by the normal pin to fire the bomb when in the short range role, but experience soon showed that this was a refinement too far. Soldiers often dropped the fitment into the barrel upside down, so that the firing pin would not work, or they forgot to pick it up when they moved and thus lost it. Ballistically, there were problems with accuracy due to inconsistent velocities and chamber pressures. The bomb was redesigned with a two-part charge system, and the insert system was abandoned. For short ranges the bomb is fired with only the primary cartridge; for the full range the secondary cartridge is clipped around the tail.

The bombs are of a highly advanced design; the first HE bomb was of aluminium but with a coiled, notched wire lining which, when the filling detonated, was shattered into several thousand fragments. This proved to be too expensive and complex to manufacture, and in 1992 was replaced by a bomb with a plain body of spheroidal graphited cast iron. Smoke and illuminating bombs are also provided.

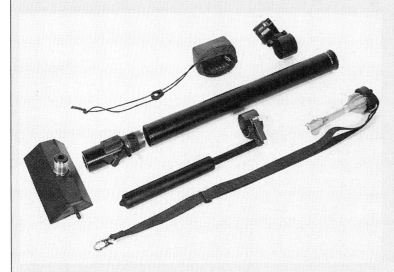

The original 51mm mortar, with monopod. The short-range insert is on the far right, at the end of the sling.

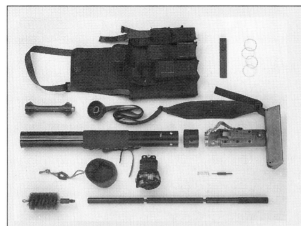

The final production version of the 51mm mortar, reduced to its component parts. The monopod has gone, a cleaning brush has been added, and the short-range insert is still present.

The 51mm mortar assembled and with the sight in place.

Firing the 51mm mortar is a one-man affair.

give a lower-powered charge for short ranges, but the very low, very short-range proposal was quietly forgotten.

But the British adoption of the 51mm mortar seems to have triggered off a demand for light and simple platoon weapons, and a host of designs appeared in the 1970s; almost always of 60mm calibre, most had some form of simple bipod which allowed a degree of control over the elevation by simply moving the legs closer to or further away from the tube. Then came the rather bright idea of simply attaching a sling to the basic tube, and providing it with a rudimentary spade at the bottom. The sling, though, was rather tougher and wider than usual and carried a number of metal tags across its width. These tags were labelled with ranges in hundreds of metres, and all the soldier had to do was drop the mortar on its spade, tilt the barrel so that the sling lay partly on the ground, and then put his boot on the sling so that the edge of his boot lay against his desired range tag. The soldier then pulled up on the muzzle to tighten the sling, which produced the correct elevation for the desired range.

The Hotchkiss-Brandt 60mm 'proximity mortar', designed to be brought into action rapidly and operated in the simplest possible manner when in close proximity to the enemy.

Presumably the soldier would have been reminded to lean back a bit before dropping the bomb into the muzzle. Generally called 'Commando' mortars, some have a more scientific method of obtaining the range, by using a spirit level with a curved bubble tube – move the barrel until the bubble is opposite the chosen range and the elevation is set.

And, moving from Commando to heavier mortars, it is worth remembering that although mortars are almost always moved by some form of automotive power these days, they are still designed so that they can be man-carried, with the three basic components – barrel, bipod and baseplate – all being designed so as to be within

A Turkish 60mm 'Commando' mortar, about as basic as you can get.

Three South African Commando mortars; two have the curved spirit level method of setting the elevation, the third has the sling with range tags. All use a simple white line on the barrel for giving direction.

A variation on the curved spirit level is this Israeli 60mm mortar, where a simple bubble tube is rotated on a frame to the desired range and then the mortar is elevated to centre the bubble.

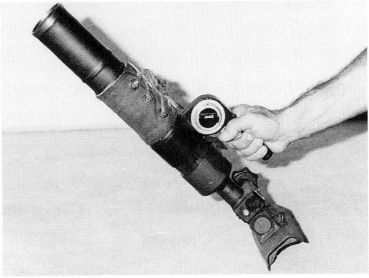

The great virtue of the Commando pattern mortar is that one man can easily carry it in addition to his personal weapon and equipment. This is the Spanish Ecia 60mm Commando.

the carrying power of one man (although one is inclined to think that some designers have an optimistic view of what constitutes a man-load). As a result, there have been extensive trials in the USA and possibly elsewhere into the feasibility of using ceramic materials to provide a barrel of the desired strength but weighing much less than a barrel of the usual steel. A ceramic 120mm tube reinforced with an outer layer of carbon-fibre was displayed some years ago in the USA but it seems that trials are still in progress.

SELF-PROPULSION

The last quarter of the twentieth century saw a rapid increase in what I call 'infantry armour' – armoured personnel carriers, mechanized infantry combat vehicles, infantry fighting vehicles – all of which have the effect of putting the infantryman on tracks or wheels and behind armour. And, of course, his equipment goes with him, including his mortars. This might not seem a new idea – we have already discussed the wartime American vehicles, and the British carted their 3in around strapped to a Bren Gun Carrier – but most of the wartime vehicles were simply a means of getting the standard mortar to

Once the mortar increases in size, the task of manhandling becomes a little more difficult. This is the Spanish 81mm model L mortar ready for the road. No prizes for guessing which one is the NCO in charge.

But once you get to the 120mm category, things become more burdensome; the Argentine soldier on the left is carrying 44kg (97lb) of 120mm mortar barrel and the man in the middle has 45kg of baseplate.

You can *man-pack the Spanish 120mm mortar, but the makers thoughtfully provide a little cart which takes everything.*

And the Israelis wisely do not attempt to man-carry their 160mm, but provide it with a carriage which doubles as the firing mounting.

The Israeli 160mm mortar in firing order, complete with a hydraulic recoil system and using the wheels to give very fast and easy traverse.

where it was wanted, whereupon it was off-loaded and put in action on the ground.

However, if great pains are being taken to protect the man, it follows that the weapon should be protected as well. This led to the development of modified mortars which could be fired from inside the armoured vehicle. In practice, this has turned out to be fairly straightforward: the usual solution is to place a turntable on the floor of the vehicle upon which the mortar and its bipod are mounted; the mortar locks into the turntable as if

it were the baseplate. The mortar can then fire out through a hatch placed above it and can, by use of the turntable, shoot in any direction, not demanding that the vehicle be aligned in any particular way.

A more specialized and luxurious solution is to develop a special mortar to be built into the vehicle, and the easiest way to do this is to adopt tank technology and put the mortar into a turret so as to give it full traverse. Very few designs have been done in this way, however, as it has

What do you do with a tank when it is outclassed as a fighting vehicle but still sound in wind and limb? If you are an Israeli soldier you hack it about and fit your 160mm mortar into it.

The British Army developed a special mounting for its 81mm mortar in APCs.

A simple solution to mortar mobility is to modify the normal bipod mounting and fit the thing into the floor of your standard armoured personnel carrier. A French 81mm mortar in an Acmat armoured truck.

The Spanish have this neat turntable unit which can be anchored into the floor of virtually any vehicle.

The Israeli Army also believes in the turntable solution

One of the more luxurious solutions is this 120mm Soltam mortar mounted in a Mowag Piranha armoured carrier. This particular model was being tried by the Israeli Army.

At the other end of the scale is this simple Swedish solution.

A low-powered Brandt 60mm gun-mortar mounted in a Panhard armoured car.

The more powerful 60mm long-range gun-mortar in the larger Panhard reconnaissance vehicle.

This picture, rescued from an old file, is marked '2 inch mortar sight; Drawing E/2661, September 1942 SECRET'. Well, it obviously would not do for the enemy to get his hands on such advanced technology, would it?

generally been felt that mounting the mortar on the turntable under the hatch is quite adequate and a good deal cheaper.

One firm, however, carried the idea a stage further. Thomson-Brandt of France devised the 'gun-mortar' for mounting in armoured cars and similar vehicles. Just as a gun-howitzer combines the high velocity of a gun with the multiple charges and high trajectory of a howitzer, so the gun-mortar can fire at high velocity and low elevations to act as a conventional gun, or it can be elevated to fire like a conventional mortar. In the gun role it is breech-loaded with a fixed round (cartridge and projectile in one piece) and some can develop sufficient velocity to make it worthwhile to fire discarding sabot armour-piercing ammunition. In the mortar role it can be breech-loaded with a conventional mortar round, or, if the climate outside is equable, then the gunner can stand in the turret hatch and drop the bombs down the muzzle in the normal mortar fashion. The idea was copied in South Africa and other countries, and there is no doubt that it provides a very versatile armament for light reconnaissance vehicles.

Soviet Superheavy Mortars

160mm Mortar M160

Calibre	160mm (6.24in)
Barrel length	4.55m (14ft 11in)
Weight in action	1,300kg (2,866lb)
Elevation	+ 50 degrees to + 80 degrees
Weight of bomb	41.5kg (91.5lb)
Muzzle velocity	343m/sec (1,125ft/sec)
Minimum range	750m (820yd)
Maximum range	8,040m (8,796yd)

The Soviets originally adopted a 160mm mortar in 1943, seeking to provide their infantry divisions with a highly destructive weapon which would be easily transportable, simple to use and cheap to manufacture. The long barrel meant that muzzle loading was impractical, and an ingenious breech-loading system was adopted, in which the barrel tips forward on the trunnions so as to bring the breech up to a convenient position for loading. The weapon was widely used and in post-war years was distributed to or copied by most of the Communist-aligned nations.

The design was overhauled in the early 1960s and emerged with an even longer barrel, which increased the maximum range from 5,150m to 8,040m (5,635–8,795yd). The bomb was also improved, making it from higher-grade steel and hence with greater explosive content. This new M160 model replaced the wartime models in Warsaw Pact countries and was also supplied to several fellow-travellers in various parts of the world.

The M160 mortar in the travelling mode. It is brought into action by simply tipping it back onto its baseplate and then running the wheels forward to act as the barrel support.

Soviet Superheavy Mortars *continued*

240mm Mortar M240

Calibre	240mm (9.36in)
Barrel length	5.34m (17ft 6in)
Weight in action	n/a
Elevation	+ 45 degrees to + 65 degrees
Weight of bomb	130kg (286.7lb)
Muzzle velocity	n/a
Minimum range	800m (875yd)
Maximum range	9,700m (10,612yd)
Rate of fire	1rd/min

The Russian 240mm M240 mortar is generally seen as a scaled-up version of the successful 160mm models.

This was first known outside Russia in 1953, and is classed as artillery rather than as an infantry support weapon, being allotted to heavy artillery brigades as a demolition weapon for use against fortification and other defensive works.

As with the 160mm weapon, the barrel swings down to allow the bomb to be loaded via the breech, and the barrel moved in a cradle with two hydro-pneumatic recoil cylinders; it shows a remarkable similarity to a 22cm mortar that the Czech Skoda factory was developing for the German Army when the war ended in 1945.

The mortar is brought into action in a similar manner to the 160mm, by lowering the baseplate to the ground and then using the wheels and suspension as the forward support for the barrel. Numbers of these mortars were supplied to Egypt, Romania and Syria, and the most recent information indicates that they have now probably been retired from front-line service and placed in the reserve. In Russian service they were replaced by a self-propelled 240mm howitzer in the early 1990s.

This rare picture of an experimental Skoda 22cm mortar of 1944/45 has some points of similarity with the later Russian design.

Thomson-Brandt 120mm rifled

Mortar, 120mm, Mle MO-120-RT

Calibre	120mm (4.7in)
Barrel length	2.06m (81in)
Weight in action	582kg (1283lb)
Elevation	+30 degrees to + 85 degrees
Weight of bomb	18.6kg (41lb)
Muzzle velocity	240m/s (787ft/s)
Minimum range	1,100m (1,200yd)
Maximum range	8,135m (8,900yd)

This is a heavy weapon which has a performance comparable to a field gun; with the standard bomb it reaches to 8,135m, but with a rocket-assisted bomb it can range to 13,000m (14,220yd). There is also a special long-range bomb which uses a plastic obturating ring, does not take the rifling, is fin-stabilized and rocket-assisted and can reach to 17,000m (18,600yd).

The mortar is unusual in that it can only fire off its wheels, since they form the front support when in the firing position. Traverse is by moving the barrel cradle across the axle, a favourite technique of French designers, and elevation is done coarsely by altering the position of the cradle relative to the axle, and finely by altering the position of the barrel within the cradle, using the barrel cooling fins as a form of rack-and-pinion adjustment.

The baseplate is a massive casting and is 'planted' into the ground by firing a 'bedding-in' bomb before commencing fire for effect. This bedding-in round can be a conventional fin-stabilized bomb for the smooth-bore 120mm mortar; these can also be fired for effect if the supply of rifled bombs runs short, but do not achieve the same range or accuracy.

The barrel is rifled with forty grooves, and the bombs are provided with copper driving bands pre-engraved with forty grooves, so that the bomb has to be carefully fitted into the rifling when muzzle-loading. This is less difficult than it sounds and it is possible to reach a rate of fire of eighteen rounds per minute for short periods and maintain a steady rate of twelve rounds per minute.

The Brandt 120mm rifled mortar as made under licence in Turkey as the MKEK HY-12.

Thomson-Brandt 120mm rifled *continued*

Rear view of the Brandt 120mm rifled mortar, showing how the mortar traverses across the axle.

The MO-120-RT on tow behind a Lohr 'light airmobile vehicle'. Presumably the crew sit on top of the ammunition.

Things have come on a little since 1942; this is the Canadian M64A1 mortar sight, made by no less a firm than Leitz of the Leica camera fame.

FIRE CONTROL

The electronic revolution of the 1960s and 1970s also had its effect upon the way mortars were directed. In its early days the mortar was used at ranges where the mortar squad could see the target and correct fire on to it, the first round being estimated by judging the range (or, more usually, making an inspired guess) and setting the elevation accordingly and then heaving the barrel and bipod around until an eye across the barrel gave the right line. Then the effect of enemy fire led the mortar into concealed positions, and so the standard techniques of indirect fire had to be applied, although they were considerably simplified.

Using a map, the position of the mortar was identified and the general location of the enemy, so that a line of fire could be determined. This was laid out on the ground using two markers and a compass, and the mortar was then placed in action with the barrel pointing along this line. A suitable aiming mark was chosen and the mortar sight pointed at it, locked and set at zero. When a target was found, the line relative to this 'zero line' was quickly plotted and the deviation in degrees set on the sight. By traversing the mortar until the sight once more pointed at the aiming mark the barrel had been pointed at the target area and the first bomb could be fired. Thereafter an observer reported where the bomb fell in relation to the target and the mortar commander deduced corrections, based upon his own experience and practice, to bring the bomb onto the desired spot. As might be imagined, there was a certain element of luck involved, and a rather greater element of sheer acquired skill. A good mortar commander had an intuitive relationship with his mortar and knew just how much to turn which handle to achieve the result he wanted.

When the new generation of mortars began to appear in the 1960s, they had far greater range, which meant that the primitive methods of yore were no longer acceptable. The infantry was going to have to start thinking about forward observers, communications from the observer to the mortar, improved ranging techniques, meteorological effects and several other factors which had hitherto been strictly artillery affairs. They were still contemplating all this when the pocket calculator came into existence and some ingenious soldiers realized that they could do some very simple trigonometry on these devices that would provide them with very accurate bearing and range from the mortar to the target, provided they could map-fix the two points with

Fly-K

Fly-K Individual Weapon System TN-8111

Calibre	52mm (2.03in)
Barrel length	605mm (23.6in)
Weight in action	4.5kg (9lb 14oz)
Elevation	+40 degrees to +85 degrees
Weight of bomb	765g (27oz)
Muzzle velocity	88.5m/sec (290ft/sec)
Minimum range	200m (219yd)
Maximum range	700m (766yd)

Firing the FLY-K 52mm mortar

The operating principle of the FLY-K, showing how the captive piston launches the bomb but confines the noise and flash.

This unusual weapon was first seen in 1983, since when it has changed hands, vanished, reappeared, and was finally adopted by the French Marines in the middle 1990s. Its most apparent feature is its compactness and low weight; what is not immediately apparent is its undetectable operation.

Fly-K is a modified form of spigot mortar; it has what appears to be a conventional barrel but is actually only a guide tube and is of light construction. Inside this is a long spigot with a firing pin at the top. The tail of the bomb carries a patented propulsion unit.

When the bomb is dropped into the guide tube, the spigot passes up inside the tail until it hits a cartridge at the forward end of the tail tube. This explodes and drives a tight-fitting piston down the tail tube, thus thrusting against the tip of the spigot and launching the bomb into the air. As the piston reaches the end of the tail tube it is arrested and locked, so retaining all the combustion gases inside the tail of the bomb. There is, therefore, no noise due to the escape of the gases, and no heating effect, flash or fumes to be detected by infra-red. In absolutely silent conditions it is just possible to hear a dull thud as the mortar is fired, if you are close to it. But in the normal conditions of the battlefield, it is virtually impossible that an enemy could be alerted before the bombs are bursting around him.

The design first appeared using modified rifle grenades as the bombs, but a completely fresh range of ammunition was then developed and HE-fragmentation, smoke/incendiary, illuminating and practice bombs are now available. There is also a multi-barrelled version, with twelve spigots mounted on a baseplate which can be ground-emplaced or fitted into a vehicle.

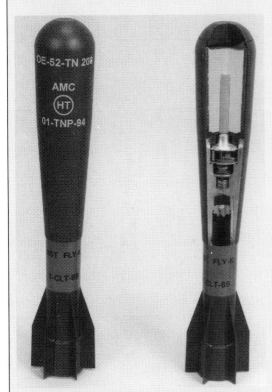

The high-explosive bomb for the FLY-K mortar, with a sectioned specimen showing the captive piston at the end of the tail tube.

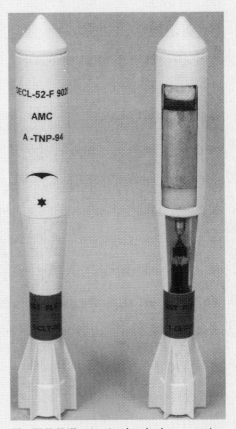

The FLY-K illuminating bomb, demonstrating that there is enough room for a conventional parachute flare in the small warhead.

reasonable accuracy. Some soldiers even went as far as to write to the major computer companies to ask whether they could develop chips for these pocket calculators which would perform various artillery-related calculations, since by this time large-sized computers were in service to provide fire-control data and what the ingenious gunners wanted was a back-up system for when the 'official' computer failed. This alerted the computer wizards, and by the late 1970s several hand-held computing devices were being field tested, resulting in a number of them coming into use in various countries in the early 1980s. And when this was followed by the widespread issue of position-finding equipment using satellite technology, accurate fire control was now well within the reach of infantry mortar squads since it could be achieved by a single hand-held instrument that could firstly locate the mortar to within 10m, calculate the bearing and range to a target, then calculate firing data – elevation, range, charge and fuze-setting – and even keep a running tally of how many rounds had been fired on what target.

In fact, there is a practical limit to the accuracy you can use. Although experimental mortar fire-control computers have been made to incorporate ballistic corrections for meteorological conditions, I am reasonably certain that no army employs them. In the first place, it would demand a new infrastructure to acquire and distribute the necessary information every four hours, because the data demanded by tube artillery is not the same as that which would be demanded by mortars. And in the second place, as many savants have discovered in the past, it is possible to take your calculations to a degree of accuracy which exceeds anything the weapon can provide, because the Law of Probabilities has a certain amount of say in the performance of any weapon. If the probable error of a system is a 100m circle there is little point in demanding a computing system accurate to 5m. Moreover, there are still a few quirks of guns and mortars which defy analysis by the scientists; gunnery still has its mysteries and is far from being as cut and dried as the boffins would like you to believe.

But given that a very fair degree of accuracy in plotting and calculation can be achieved and the firing data can now be calculated with a fine degree of accuracy it does therefore follow that the sight on the mortar should be capable of using as much of that accuracy as possible. The first mortars merely had a white line painted down the middle of the barrel to indicate direction, and a pendulum arranged alongside a scale of degrees of elevation. The mortar commander had a plumb-line, and to take aim he stood where he could see the target – or an aiming stake in the target's direction – and held his plumb bob up in front of his eye, lining up the plumb line, the mortar and the target. He then had his crew shift

and swivel the mortar until the white line on the barrel was aligned with his plumb line, and that was the direction taken care of. He also had a card with elevations equivalent to ranges, and this was applied by elevating the barrel until the pendulum cut the scale at the appropriate figure. The mortar was laid.

Then came the 'goniometric sight', simply a sighting vane capable of rotating on a scale of degrees. This could be pointed at an aiming mark, as previously described, and by setting off the degree scale the mortar could be laid on lines determined from a map. Later still, in the 1930s,

This South African mortar/machine gun sight is a 'collimating' sight, using a quasi-optical sighting tube which displays an aiming mark superimposed upon the view seen when both eyes are open. Cheaper than an optical system and, if properly made, as this one obviously is, no less accurate.

The sight unit for the Swiss 60mm mortar has a number of range scales for use with different bombs; this shows the scale for the illuminating bomb.

A Russian soldier using a simple goniometric sight during World War II.

AND NEXT . . .

And so we have entered the twenty-first century with the mortar a firmly established weapon in the military inventory. In the course of the twentieth century it has gone from being a military oddity to a highly sophisticated and accurate weapon. Modern computer technology has produced small hand-held fire-control computers which can even link into the global positioning system of satellites and thereafter calculate firing data for targets with a degree of accuracy that fifty years ago would have been deemed impossible. And the mortars can actually fire to that degree of accuracy. Their projectiles have an effect – be it fragmentation, blast, smoke clouds or illumination – that is greatly improved over what the mortars of fifty years ago could achieve.

And if you ask me what is coming next, I have to tell you that I do not know, for the very good reason that I cannot think of anything you might wish to do with a mortar that you cannot do

the 'collimating sight' came into fashion. This was similar to the goniometric sight but instead of a simple open sighting vane it had a tube with an optical element inside it which, when looked at from some distance, displayed a white triangle or arrow or line. The mortarman kept both eyes open and moved his mortar until the white marker was superimposed upon the target or the aiming mark.

Finally, in the 1960s, the new and improved mortars demanded new and improved sights and artillery-style dial (or panoramic) sights were adopted, with full optical systems in which the layer looked to see a set of cross-wires which he laid on his aiming mark. One of the greatest advantages of these sights, in addition to greater accuracy, was that the cross-wires could be illuminated so as to make night firing a great deal easier.

This portable computer by Dassault of France can perform all the required gunnery and meteorological calculations, store up to ninety-nine targets and control up to ninety-nine mortars.

A British mortar squad, firing from an APC, has its firing data produced by the Morzen hand-held computer

A Norwegian mortar squad using a British 81mm mortar with the 'Hugin' fire control system which links observers, commanders and firing teams in a radio data transmission system.

perfectly well right now. So where the improvement is coming from is very difficult to imagine. It is probable that the mortar has reached a similar plateau of excellence that currently carries the infantryman's assault rifle: it is so good that attempts to improve it would be so difficult and expensive as to be not worth the effort.

6 Mortar Ammunition

As a generalization, we could say that mortar ammunition follows the same design principles as artillery ammunition, with a few digressions here and there to suit particular weapons, but that is about as far as it would be wise to generalize. In its early days, mortar ammunition was characterized by being simple, cheap and un-spun, but this ceased to be the case once the Americans introduced their 4.2in rifled mortar, and mortar ammunition has increased in complexity (and cost) tenfold in the final quarter of the twentieth century.

The mortar bomb, from the sixteenth to the nineteenth centuries, changed but little. It was a hollow spherical cast-iron bomb with a hole through which gunpowder or other substances were inserted, and the hole then closed with a wooden time fuze. The fuze was simply a tapering beechwood peg with a central hole drilled through it and a recess in the top end. The hole and the recess were filled with a paste made from fine gunpowder and 'spirits of wine'. When dry, this formed an impervious filling which, when ignited, burned at a fairly regular rate; I say 'fairly regular', since checking this rate, before the invention of stopwatches and accurate timekeeping, was a matter of burning a fixed length and seeing how many times the Apostle's Creed could be recited before it burned out. The peg was then marked off in arbitrary divisions, and it became part of the gunner's art to know what division marked the point at which the peg was to be cut short so as to leave the head end and the right length of powder to burst the shell at the desired range. Having made the cut, the peg was driven into the shell, and the end, until then protected by a tarred cloth cover, was exposed. On firing the shell, the flash of the propelling charge ignited the powder in the recessed head of the fuze, and this in turn ignited the central stem of powder. This burned away during flight, and if the gunner had got his calculation right, the contents of the shell would be ignited just as the shell arrived at or over the target.

The contents of the shell were usually gunpowder mixtures in order to shatter the shell and shower the enemy with fragments; the only other real alternative was an incendiary mixture, and these varied according to the fancies of the firemaster and the availability of inflammable substances. Resin, turpentine, sulphur, tallow, various nitrates, indeed virtually anything that would burn fiercely would be compounded so that, once lit by the fuze, they would burn violently and strew blazing pieces in all directions to set houses and structures on fire. Some were compounded with substances that gave more light than fire and were used to illuminate an area at night, being particularly useful in sieges when the activities of escalading parties and sappers could be detected and dealt with.

The arrival of the trench mortar in 1915 saw the beginnings of improvement upon these primitive devices, although it has to be said that some of the first 1915–16 projectiles were rather more primitive than their forebears.

The first bomb for the Stokes mortar, for example, was no more than a cast-iron cylinder with a bourrelet machine at each end. (A bourrelet is a belt of metal machined very carefully to the correct bore diameter minus windage on an otherwise roughly finished body of rather smaller diameter. It saves machining time by not dealing with the whole surface of the bomb body, but provides the necessary accurate surfaces to ride in the bore and centralize the bomb.) At the rear end

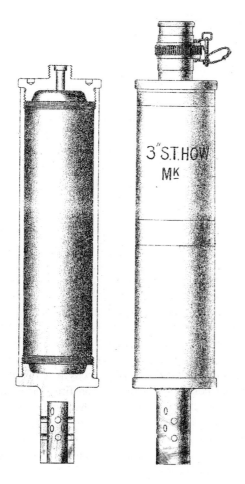

The Stokes 3in mortar bomb of 1915, with an 'all-ways' fuze which was a slight improvement over the original 'pistol' design.

The bomb for the 4in Stokes mortar, fitted with a time fuze so as to burst the bomb in the air and drench the target with gas.

of this cylinder was a perforated tube into which the propellant cartridge was inserted, and at the front end there was a 'pistol' – which was an archaic term indicating a fuze which delivered a detonation rather than ignition to the contents of the projectile. In fact, it was the working parts of the No. 5 Mills Grenade – the familiar fly-off lever, spring-loaded striker, cap, fuze and detonator – simply attached to a metal stalk which screwed into the front end of the bomb. A clip held the fly-off lever in place, and the initial

acceleration of the bomb caused the clip to 'set back' and release the lever; this rode on the inside of the bore until it reached the muzzle, where it flew off and released the striker to fire the cap, which lit the short length of time fuze, which eventually fired the detonator to set off the explosive inside the bomb.

Primitive as this device was, it shows the three essentials of any mortar bomb (or, indeed, any round of ammunition): the bomb, the propelling charge and the fuze. There is a fourth require-

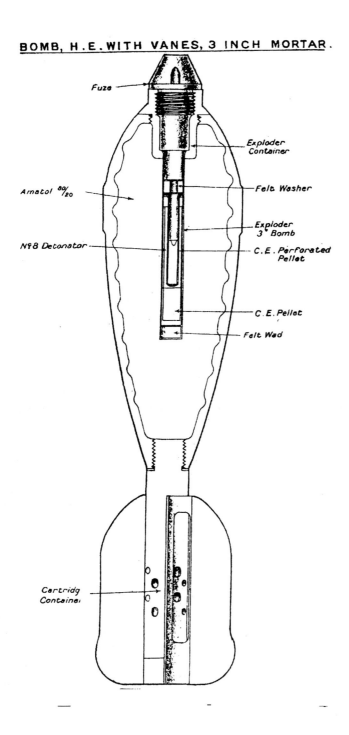

BOMB, H.E. WITH VANES, 3 INCH MORTAR.

Fuze

Exploder Container

Amatol 80/20

Felt Washer

Exploder 3" Bomb

Nº8 Detonator

C.E. Perforated Pellet

C.E. Pellet

Felt Wad

Cartridg Container

One of the early finned bombs for the 3in Stokes mortar. Note that the interior of the bomb body is grooved, vertically as well as horizontally, so as to form planes of weakness to assist in breaking into the desired size of fragment. An early and very effective way of controlling fragmentation.

ment, which Stokes ignored: a means of stabilizing the flight of the bomb so that it follows a regular and repeatable trajectory. The Stokes bomb, fired from a smooth-bore mortar with no system of stabilization, simply tumbled end over end as it went through the air, although for all that it usually managed to land close to the intended target.

Like every bomb that followed it for many years, the first Stokes bomb was of cast iron, firstly because it was cheap and secondly because it was brittle and would break up into reasonable fragments without demanding extremely powerful (plus expensive and scarce) high explosives. The body was strong enough to withstand the acceleration as it left the bore, with a little over for the sake of safety, and the explosive inside was whatever could be spared from the munitions programme, which meant amatol, ammonal, baratol or one of the many adulterated high explosives which were used in the first half of World War I in order to take advantage of as many sources of supply as possible.

The propelling charge for the Stokes was no more than a 12-bore shotgun cartridge filled with Ballistite (a Nobel patented smokeless powder, very fast-burning) and except for some minor changes in the composition of the explosive this has more or less stayed the same since Stokes's day. The only serious difference is that once mortars grew more powerful there was not sufficient room inside a 12-bore cartridge case for the amount of propellant needed, and various methods had to be employed to provide the extra power. This led to the separation of the charge into two components, the 'primary' cartridge and the 'secondary' cartridges. The primary cartridge was the shotgun case, with the cap and Ballistite loading, inserted into the hollow tail unit of the bomb. When the bomb is dropped down the bore, the cartridge cap strikes the firing pin, or, according to the chosen firing system, the bomb comes to rest at the bottom of the bore and the firing pin is then released to fire the cap. The secondaries were combustible containers attached

to the outside of the tail unit so that the flash of the primary firing, which passed through holes in the tail unit, would ignite the secondaries to provide the explosion which would send the bomb to the desired range.

The nature of the secondary cartridge takes various forms. Perhaps the simplest was that seen on the American 4.2in and some others, in which sheets of nitro-cellulose powder where stitched together in bundles, pierced with a large hole the diameter of the tail boom, and slotted down one side, so that the bundle could be slipped around the tail boom. This has the advantage that individual sheets of propellant could be torn off to fine-tune the charge, but naked propellant is prone to deterioration from damp and can be something of a hazard if the torn-off sheets are not disposed of carefully.

A more usual system is to prepare sheets of powder in a horseshoe shape and then enclose them in some combustible cloth, so that the resulting flexible package can be slipped around the tail boom above the fins. Where the propellant powder is granulated, as in the British 81mm mortar, then the loose grains can be poured into a horseshoe-shaped celluloid container and clipped around the tail.

The British 3in and 4.2in, among others, used cylindrical celluloid containers filled with granulated powder, of such a diameter and length as to fit between the fins, where they were retained by a spring. Whatever the system used, the object is to provide the firer with a number of charges of progressively greater power, by adding one or more secondaries to the primary. The cartridges are designed so that there is an overlap in the range performance; thus a primary and one secondary might permit firing from 200 to 700m (220–770yd) range, according to the elevation of the barrel. The primary and two secondaries from 500 to 1,500m (550–1,650yd), the primary and three from 1,200 to 2,000m (1,315–2,190yd) and so on. This ensures that between the minimum and maximum ranges there will be no gaps in coverage and also that a fair proportion of the

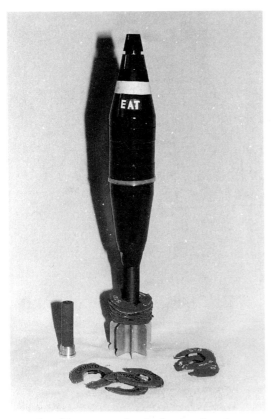

A modern 81mm mortar bomb, showing the primary cartridge and the secondaries in horseshoe form, wrapped in combustible fabric and coloured for identification of the various charge combinations.

total range covered can be reached by various combinations of elevation and charge so that it is rare for an intervening crest to pose any problem for a well-designed mortar.

The fuze was the most difficult area of all in the early mortars. The time fuze used with the first Stokes bombs was chosen simply because there was no guarantee of what attitude the bomb might be in when it landed, and thus is was impossible to use a normal artillery-type impact fuze screwed into the nose. Moreover, artillery fuzes by 1915 were invariably designed so that they were safe up to and during firing and then were 'armed' during flight so that they arrived at the target ready to function. This arming was invariably

done by a combination of violent acceleration and rapid spin, neither of which were present in the early mortar bombs.

Eventually, when finned bombs gave an assurance of the front end arriving first, an impact fuze was practicable, though it was perhaps the most primitive fuze ever invented. The 'Newton Fuze' or Fuze, Percussion, No. 110, according to the official introduction, 'consists of a conical steel housing carrying a needle disc over a converted .303 cartridge case. Instantaneous or delay cartridges are provided.'; the rifle cartridge case was simply filled with a suitable gunpowder charge, with or without a delay element, and the housing was screwed into the head of the bomb. Immediately before firing, the needle disc – simply a spring steel cap with a sharp spike in it – was lifted, the cartridge slipped into place in the central boring in the housing, and the needle disc replaced. On firing, the spring of the steel resisted the effects of acceleration, and when the bomb landed nose-first the needle was driven into the cap of the cartridge and it all happened. The delay element was for use when the enemy was beneath light cover – a corrugated iron roof or a layer of sandbags, for example – the impact with the cover would ignite the delay, the bomb would continue on its way through the cover and a fraction of a second after impact, just as the bomb emerged underneath the cover, it exploded.

An alternative approach was to invent a fuze which would go off on impact no matter how the bomb landed. This trick can be achieved by putting a lead ball between two hollow coned faces, and having a firing pin on the other side of one of these faces. The fuze screws into the bomb nose. If the bomb lands on its nose, then a detonator is flung forward by the sudden stop and strikes the firing pin, setting off the bomb. If the bomb lands sideways, the lead ball is driven to one side, forcing the two cones apart and driving the firing pin into the detonator. If the bomb lands on its tail, then the lead ball hammers the firing pin into the detonator. The only problem left is how to stop the thing going off when you fire the

The Newton Fuze, the principal component of which was a .303in blank cartridge, slightly modified.

FUZE, PERCUSSION, Nº 110, MK. III |L|.

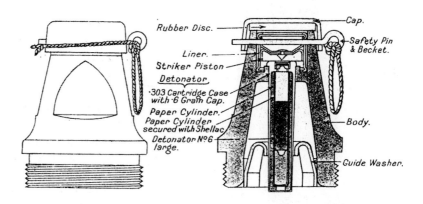

Rubber Disc.
Liner.
Striker Piston
Detonator.
·303 Cartridge Case with ·6 Grain Cap.
Paper Cylinder.
Paper Cylinder secured with Shellac.
Detonator Nº6 large.

Cap.
Safety Pin & Becket.
Body.
Guide Washer.

The 'all-ways' fuze; no matter how it landed the momentum of the lead ball would force the two coned portions outwards and drive the needle into the detonator, or drive the detonator onto the needle.

FUZE, PERCUSSION, SPIGOT, Nº 148, MK. I |L|.

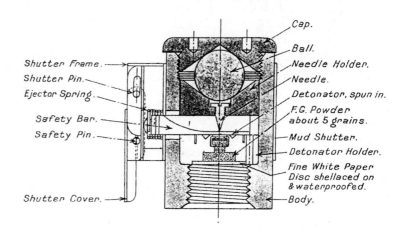

Shutter Frame.
Shutter Pin.
Ejector Spring.
Safety Bar.
Safety Pin.
Shutter Cover.

Cap.
Ball.
Needle Holder.
Needle.
Detonator, spun in.
F.G. Powder about 5 grains.
Mud Shutter.
Detonator Holder.
Fine White Paper Disc shellaced on & waterproofed.
Body.

bomb and it suddenly accelerates, and there are various ways of doing this.

Stability of flight with smooth-bore mortars was achieved by putting fins on the tail of the bomb. This seems so obvious now that one wonders how anybody could have made bombs without fins, but in 1915 there was no precedent. Scarcely anybody had made a projectile with tail fins, and those who had developed such designs had never seen much success, largely because

they were proposing their use with rifled weapons, where they showed no advantage. But once the idea was tried with a mortar bomb it rapidly spread until by 1917 it was unthinkable to have a bomb without fins.

The eventual shape of the smooth-bore mortar bomb settled down to one of two patterns: either a cylindrical bomb, or a teardrop-shaped one, both with a cluster of fins. But within that broad grouping there were some fine old idiosyncrasies

FUZE, TIME, Nº 79, MK. II [L].

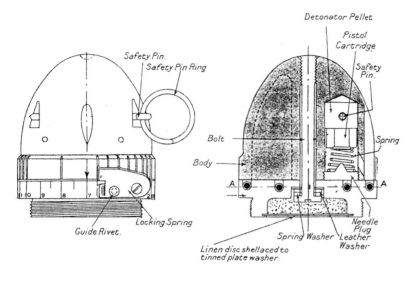

A simple time fuze of 1917; a length of lead-covered powder fuze is laid in a groove in the base. In the dome is a detonator pellet and beneath it a needle. To set the fuze, the dome is turned on the base until the arrow points to the desired time, and a spike is then driven through the vertical hole above the arrow so as to puncture the lead fuze. On firing, the detonator pellet sets back onto the needle and fires the detonator. This flash, inside the dome, ignites the powder in the fuze through the punched hole. The powder burns in both directions; one leads to a dead end, the other leads to the fuze magazine in the base and ignites it, so exploding the contents of the bomb.

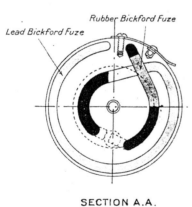

SECTION A.A.

loose, largely because the science of aerodynamics was in its infancy and partly because the primary thought uppermost in the designer's mind was 'keep it cheap'. An expensive bomb would have no chance, because cheapness and simplicity were the bedrock of the mortar philosophy.

The cylindrical bomb was found where the size of the payload was more important than the maximum range; gas was a prominent example of

this. The usual range required of a gas bomb was little more than across the width of no man's land, but the primary demand was to liberate the maximum quantity of gas in the minimum possible time. The ultimate of this philosophy was the Livens Projector, although the bomb in that weapon had no pretence whatever towards aerodynamic qualities or ballistic refinement. The teardrop or 'streamlined' bomb was found where range was more important than payload; in other

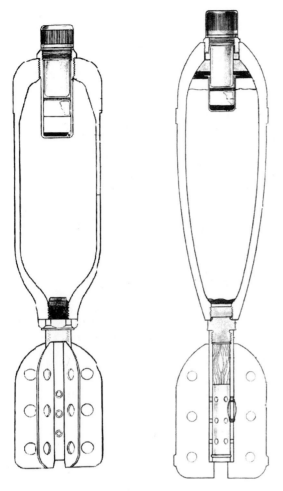

A comparison between (left) the cylindrical and (right) the streamlined designs of bomb, in this case for the British 4.2 inch mortar.

commented on the particularly deadly lethality of their bombs, and the layman might well ask what was so special about a mortar bomb when compared with an artillery shell? After all, the mortar bomb is a cheaper proposition, so why should it be so much more deadly? The reason lies in two characteristics of the mortar which affect the ammunition. The first is that the mortar is less highly stressed – in other words, the propelling charge is a great deal less than that for a gun of the same calibre and thus the projectile suffers less of a shock when it is launched. Because of this it is possible to make the bomb with a thinner casing and to fill it with more explosive; the average artillery shell of World War II contained something in the order of 8 to 10 per cent of its weight in explosive; thus a 35lb shell could be expected to contain about 3lb of TNT. The mortar bomb on the other hand carried more like 20 per cent; to give a concrete example, the German 10cm bomb for the Nebelwerfer weighed 16lb and carried a filling of 3.4lb of TNT, which is almost exactly 21 per cent of the total weight. It is obvious that more explosive on the target leads to a better effect.

The second characteristic is the high trajectory of the mortar, which leads to the bomb coming to the ground at a steep angle, usually about 70 degrees to the horizontal plane. An artillery gun shell usually impacts at about 30 degrees and thus much of the resulting fragmentation is either smothered by the ground immediately beneath or is harmlessly dissipated into the air above. But the mortar bomb's steep angle of arrival means that the bomb is almost standing upright when it detonates, and thus spreads its fragments around more evenly and without wasting them. Hence more lethality due to better distribution of fragments and blast.

Nevertheless, there are some things that mortars find difficult. One of the most effective methods of employing artillery fire against troops in trenches or foxholes is to employ a time fuze so that the shell bursts in the air above their heads, striking the fragments downwards so as to seek

words, for the general run of high-explosive bombs. In fact, the difference was primarily one of weight: the cylindrical bombs were invariably heavier than streamlined bombs, ergo the streamlined bomb went further. In the rare cases were there were bombs of both shapes and more or less equal weight, their difference in range was a good deal less than might be imagined. Streamlined they may have been, aerodynamic they were not.

In discussing mortars here I have often

behind cover and into trenches in a manner that a ground-burst shell cannot do. It is, of course, quite possible to fit time fuzes to mortar bombs as well, and as we have seen, the first mortars relied entirely upon time fuzes. But the basic concept of a mortar is simplicity at all costs, and the infantryman is reluctant to be bothered with firing tables and abstruse calculations to work out the fuze setting; they like to drop the bomb in and let it go without too much fussing about. Time fuzes were reluctantly acceptable in the static conditions of trench warfare, but in mobile warfare they were quite unacceptable.

In a praiseworthy attempt to have their cake and eat it too, the Germans produced a unique 'bouncing bomb' for their 81mm mortar. This resembled a conventional bomb in appearance, but the rounded nose was lightly pinned to the body, which had a blunt head and a short pyrotechnic delay fuze. The nose portion held a charge of smokeless powder and an impact fuze.

The bomb was loaded and fired in the normal manner and landed on its nose at the target. This caused the impact fuze to function and ignite the charge of smokeless powder, and the explosions sheared the retaining pins holding the nose cap in place. The nose cap was driven into the ground, but the bomb body was blown back up into the air again. At the same time the very short delay was ignited, so that when the bomb body reached a suitable height the explosive filling detonated and the bomb blew a cloud of fragments in all directions, giving a lethal airburst without the complications of a time fuze The planned height of burst was anywhere between 2m and 20m, it being difficult to be more precise due to slight variations in the burning of the delay element and also because it depended on the hardness of the

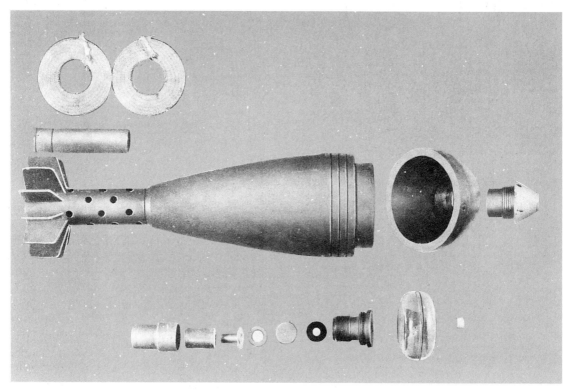

The German 81mm bouncing bomb, showing its principal components.

ground on which the bomb landed. In actual service the height of burst was usually between 6m and 15m. Provided the ground is moderately firm, this design gives a very good answer the problem, but on soft ground it tends to fail, since the bomb gets well down into the earth before the impact fuze operates and the subsequent detonation is somewhat smothered.

Today, though, the problem has been approached from a different direction, and, as you might expect, the solution is electronic. Electronic calculators can work out a fuze length in milliseconds, and electronic fuzes, which rely, fundamentally, upon a resistor-condenser timing circuit, can be charged with the timing voltage quickly and accurately so that they will burst at,

The Norwegian PPD323 multirole fuze. A quick twist of the head converts it from an impact (or 'point detonating') fuze to a radio proximity fuze, so that one fuze can perform all roles. At a price, of course.

or very close to, the desired height. Even easier for the detachment is the use of proximity fuzes. These emit a radio signal and listen for the echo to come back from the ground as the bomb nears the target. When the returning signal reaches a strength which indicates that the bomb is within lethal distance of the target, an electronic circuit closes the firing switch and the bomb detonates. The height of burst in this case tends to depend upon the reflectivity of the ground; water-soaked ground reflects the signal more strongly than does dry desert, and hence produces a higher burst. Forests, particularly wet forests, reflect the signal from the canopy of leaves and thus produce bursts that are so high as to be relatively harmless. Theoretically, it is possible to produce a spurious signal from a jammer and thus burst the bomb well away from the target, but in real life this is not an option. Fuzes can be made with a wide selection of frequencies so that some are bound to evade any jamming signal. A more significant objection to the wide use of proximity fuzes is simply the expense.

CARRIER BOMBS

The first mortar bombs were, of course, explosive anti-personnel bombs, simply intended to wreak havoc in the enemy's trenches, but it was not long before other applications suggested themselves and specialist ammunition began to appear. Gas was the first, because as the mortar began to attain some credibility, so one of the prime questions of the period was that of delivering poison gas. The mortar, short-ranging, fast-firing and with a bomb of higher capacity than any other form of weapon, appeared to be the solution.

Unfortunately for many would-be designers, there is rather more to loading a mortar bomb with gas than simply unscrewing the fuze, pouring gas in until the bomb is full, and putting the fuze back in. Poison gases are (obviously) poisonous, and therefore have to be handled under precautions. They are also almost always

141

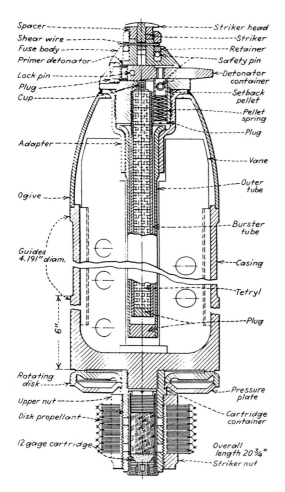

Spacer --- Striker head
Shear wire --- Striker
Fuse body --- Retainer
Primer detonator --- Safety pin
Lock pin --- Detonator container
Plug --- Setback pellet
Cup --- Pellet spring
Adapter --- Plug
--- Vane
Ogive --- Outer tube
--- Burster tube
Guides 4.191"diam. --- Casing
--- Tetryl
6" --- Plug
Rotating disk --- Pressure plate
Upper nut --- Cartridge container
Disk propellant ---
12 gage cartridge --- Overall length 20¾"
--- Striker nut

The 'chemical' shell for the US 4.2in mortar; it could be filled with war gas or with white phosphorus smoke composition. Note the internal vanes to compel the liquid filling to take up spin, the central burster tube which is just enough to split the shell open without destroying the contents, and the detail of the rotating disc and propelling charge at the rear.

highly corrosive, and react in various degrees of unpleasantness to steel or other metals, and they are often what the chemists call 'fugitive', in that they can seek out the tiniest crack and go through it – rather like red ink or anti-freeze. Consequently, the interior surfaces of bombs had to be coated with a gas-resistant varnish, or even lined with glass, and fuzes had to be protected

from contact with the liquids. Any joints in the bomb had to be sealed with adhesive compounds, the filling plug, through which the gas was loaded, had to have special sealing arrangements, and gas-detecting paint, which changed colour in the presence of certain war gases, was painted around the seams and filling plug. An air space had to be left in the bomb, so that the gas could expand and contract under climatic changes, and this, of course, meant that when the bomb was fired the gas could move, sloshing back and forth as the bomb tumbled in flight and making accurate shooting well-nigh impossible. This was particularly so with bombs fired from rifled weapons, where the liquid filling failed to take up spin at first, then picked it up and went wild and wobbled the projectile in all directions. This was countered by putting perforated divisions inside the body of the bomb, so as to impart spin to the liquid more quickly and keep it in step with the rest of the bomb, but there was nothing that could be done with an unspun bomb.

Once these problems began to come under control, the soldiers looked further afield. If gas could be carried, then how about some smoke-producing compounds, for concealing the movement of troops? This turned out to be relatively easy; almost everybody with mortars adopted white phosphorus (WP) as their smoke agent, largely because it didn't need any special fuze arrangements to ignite the smoke. All you had to so was put a small explosive charge behind the fuze, just enough to break the shell open and release the contents, whereupon the WP would ignite spontaneously when it met the air and produce a very dense cloud of white smoke. It also proved to be a useful incendiary device if the target was capable of being burned, and, of course, WP is a terrible anti-personnel weapon.

It does have one tactical drawback, however: the chemical reaction that produces the smoke also produces heat, thus warming up the surrounding air. The hot air rises – and takes the smoke with it. So you end up with a nice smokescreen about 50ft up in the air, and everybody on the ground exposed to view. This does not always happen, but it occurred often enough to make people look for some other substance. Substances such as titanium tetrachloride (FM), sulphur trioxide, chlorsulphonic acid (FS), oleum (fuming sulphuric acid) and tin tetrachloride were all tried during World War I, plus many others, and were found to produce smoke which was cooler and not so prone to rise and reveal what it was meant to be hiding, but none had the same obscuring power as WP and consequently more ammunition was needed to perform a given task.

If the user is prepared to tolerate the use of a time fuze, then special bombs carrying canisters of HC mixture, a compound of zinc oxide and hexachlorethane, can be used. The mixture has to be ignited and the canisters have to be ejected from the bomb over the required area, which makes the design complex and also poses some fire-control problems, but as a cool smoke it has the advantage of an obscuring power almost as good as WP.

A 1930s design of illuminating bomb, for the US 81mm mortar, showing the star canister, parachute and various washers and supports, all of which pack inside the bomb body.

The last type of bomb to be demanded during World War I was the illuminating bomb, to be fired over no man's land to light the area up and let the infantrymen see what the opposition was up to. Originally these were fairly primitive, simply a bomb body with a number of pyrotechnic stars inside which were ignited and then the bomb was blown open so as to allow the stars to fall through the air to the ground, emitting light as they did so. These were fairly effective but of short duration, so that a constant fire had to be kept up to provide a reasonable period of illumination.

The solution to this was to suspend the star from a parachute and thus slow its descent. And since aviation was then in its infancy, you would be excused for thinking that the parachute might not have suggested itself to the ammunition designers very quickly. But, strangely enough, the parachute preceded aviation by some time and a parachute illuminating bomb – 'Boxer's Parachute Light Ball' – was actually provided for firing from 8in mortars and howitzers as early as 1866. It therefore required no great leap of imagination to come up with a workable parachute illuminating bomb, though it took a good deal of fine-tuning before it became reliable.

The principal difficulty with illuminating bombs is to get the bomb body out of the way so that the parachute can open and control the fall of the light. A spinning artillery shell throws its components out under centrifugal force so that they spin away from the light, but a fin-stabilized bomb has to have some more positive methods applied. The most usual method is to have a time delay of some sort – or a time fuze – that ignites a small charge of black powder to blow the head off the bomb shortly after it has started on the downward leg of its flight. The flash of this charge is also employed to ignite the illuminating compound – usually a magnesium-based powder – which is pressed into an open-ended canister held in the bomb body with the open end facing the nose. The other end of the canister has a cable and parachute attached to it, the parachute being

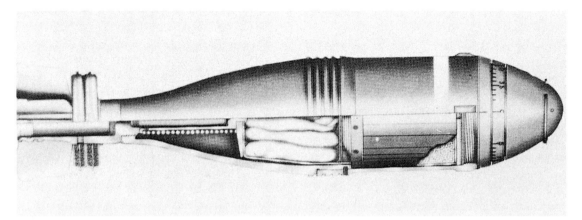

A more recent design of Yugoslavian 120mm illuminating bomb; the shape of the bomb has changed but the principle and the components remain the same. Note the coil spring in the rear of the body which ejects the contents when the time fuze blows off the nose.

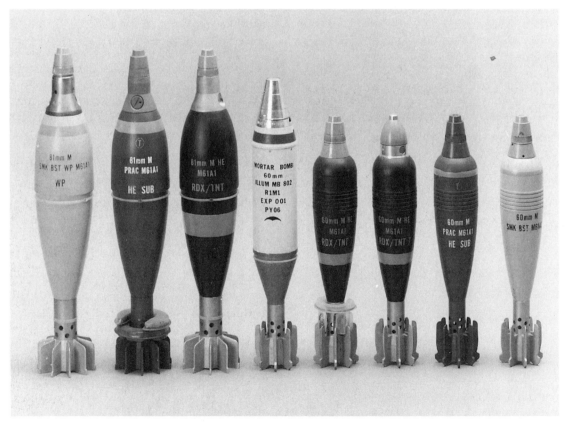

A range of South African bombs: left to right, 81mm smoke, practice and high explosive; 60mm illuminating, HE, HE, practice and smoke.

neatly folded in the tapering tail of the bomb. Behind the parachute lies a spring. So when the head is blown off the bomb, the spring is able to give the parachute and canister a push to send them out of the open nose of the bomb. The open nose then acts as a brake on the bomb and totally ruins its trajectory, so that the canister and parachute are no longer in front of the bomb and in no danger of collision. The parachute opens, the illuminating compound lights up, and the star descends relatively slowly, so that it can be expected to light up a sizeable area for perhaps one and a half to two minutes. Light strengths of up to a million candlepower are usual in modern 120mm illuminating bombs.

THE IMPROVED CONVENTIONAL MUNITION

Improved Conventional Munitions (ICM) are just what the name implies, conventional projectiles that have been improved by a bit of lateral thinking. They first appeared in 155mm artillery shells in the late 1970s, and the general form was that of a carrier shell packed with a number of

'bomblets' or mines – either anti-personnel or anti-vehicle – that was carried to the target area by the shell and there distributed. The 'bomblets' were small cylindrical munitions with a shaped charge warhead wrapped with notched steel bar or some other preformed fragmentation device, fitted with an impact fuze and with a ribbon or some similar device to ensure that they fell with the shaped charge end downwards. If they landed on armour they could make a nice hole in it, and if they hit the ground then the fragmentation sleeve meant that although the shaped charge was wasted, the detonation at least produced a cloud of anti-personnel fragments. And, of course, when they hit armour they also produced fragments. The object was to stop tanks well back from the front line; this was in the days when everybody was pointing to the Soviet superiority in armour vis-à-vis NATO and thinking up ever more desperate measures to try to equalize things.

About ten years later the Greek Powder & Cartridge Company astonished everybody by producing an ICM bomb for the US 107mm mortar, which the Greek Army had in service. Packed inside the standard-sized and shaped 4.2in bomb were twenty pre-fragmented dual-purpose

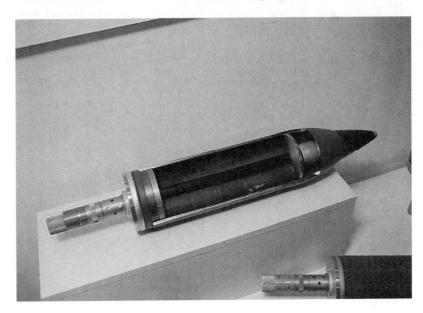

The first ICM bomb for mortars appeared in Greece in 1984 and contained shaped charge bomblets.

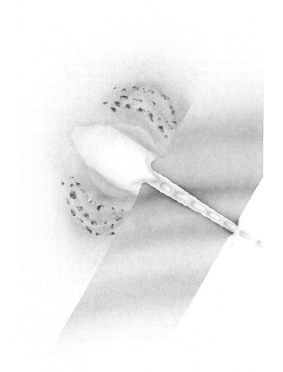

The action of the shaped charge bomblet in penetrating armour and, at the same time, generating a cloud of fragments for the anti-personnel role.

bomblets, each loaded with 30g (1oz) of high explosive. The shaped charge is capable of penetrating up to 60mm (2.3in) of armour, and the fragmentation covered an area of 15m (50ft) radius around the point of impact. The bomb is fitted with a time fuze which is set to function about 300m (330yd) above the target area. The fuze then ignites an expulsion charge which blows the rear end off the bomb and ejects the twenty bomblets. Due to the spin of the bomb, they are dispersed and will cover an area up to 140m (153yd) in diameter.

This was the answer to an infantryman's prayer – a foolproof method of keeping tanks at arm's length so that the forward lines were not swamped by armour. By engaging tanks with bomblets at ranges up to 5,500m (6,020yd) from

the mortar, the load on the anti-tank missiles and rockets operated by the forward troops could be considerably lessened. Admittedly, 60mm does not sound a great degree of armour penetration when one contemplates the current main battle tanks, but, bearing in mind that these bomblets are descending from above onto the relatively thin armour on the upper surfaces of the tank, and not attempting (like every other weapon) to go through the immensely thick frontal glacis plate or turret front, then the idea begins to look most attractive.

It certainly drew some admiring glances and before very long other designs appeared, notably a 120mm fin-stabilized bomb from Ecia of Spain which carried twenty-one bomblets of 37mm (1.4in) diameter which could defeat 150mm of armour plate and deliver 650 fragments over a lethal area of 6m (20ft) radius.

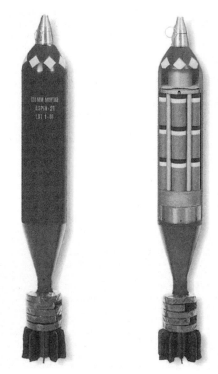

The Spanish 'Espin' 120mm ICM bomb, loaded with bomblets.

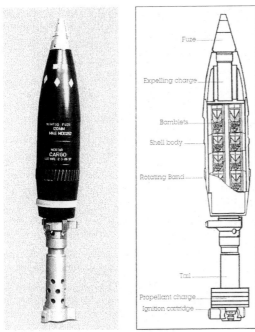

A Turkish 120mm ICM bomb for the Hotchkiss-Brandt
rifled mortar. The tail tube is blown off after launch.

LET ME BE YOUR GUIDE . . .

Copperhead

At much the same time as the ICM was first
developed for artillery, the first guided artillery
projectile appeared. This was Copperhead and its
purpose in life was, again, to deal with tanks at
extreme ranges, in this case up to 16km away from
the 155mm howitzer that fired it. This Cannon
Launched Guided Projectile (CLGP) was fired in
the same manner as an artillery shell: once it
arrived in the target area it deployed a set of fins
and wings and switched on a laser receiver in the
nose. Somewhere below, on the battlefield, some
valiant forward observer sat with a laser
designator, shining a laser beam at the target. The
Copperhead detected the stray reflections of laser
light from the target and steered itself to impact; it
had a 15lb (7kg) shaped charge inside which could
make a sizeable hole in any main battle tank.

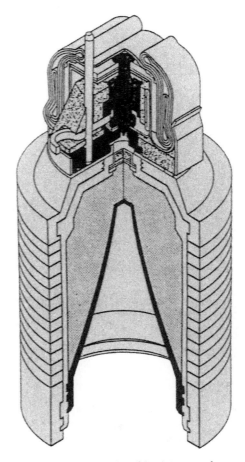

A typical dual-purpose anti-tank/anti-personnel
bomblet. The folded ribbon at the top streams out
behind when it is released so as to ensure it lands with
the shaped charge facing the target.

Copperhead was a gun projectile, but it gave
ideas to a number of designers, and since then
there have been a number of proposals and
programmes, of which four have been more or less
successful: Strix, Bussard, Merlin and FOMP.

Strix

Strix came from Sweden; it was originally
developed by FFV, the government arsenal, in
collaboration with Saab, the aircraft company, but
in later years Bofors AB took over FFV and it

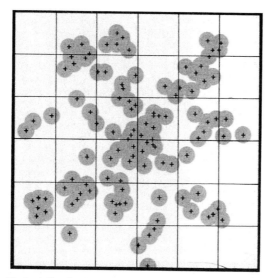

Typical distribution pattern of bomblets from five 120mm bombs. Each square is 50 × 50m, and the line of fire is straight up the centre.

became a Bofors product. Strix is formally described as an 'anti-armour guided projectile' and it is a torpedo-shaped bomb with fins wrapped around its rear end, an infra-red seeker head at the front, and a powerful shaped charge behind it. An 'after-body' with a tail fin unit, cartridge container and optional rocket booster fits on to the rear of the projectile before it is loaded in the usual manner down the muzzle of a 120mm mortar.

The cartridge fires and the entire affair is shot from the mortar. If the optional rocket motor is being used to increase the range, then the after-body stays in place until the rocket has finished its boost, after which the entire after-body falls off. If the rocket is not selected, then the after-body falls off shortly after it leaves the muzzle.

On the downward leg of the trajectory the infra-red detector switches on and begins to scan the area below the nose of the bomb. If it detects a source of heat, this is analysed and if it appears to match the signature of a tank then the computer will fire the appropriate side-thrusting rockets and steer the bomb towards the target. A proximity fuze detonates the shaped charge at the optimum distance from the tank and the resulting jet will defeat any upper surface armour in existence. The maximum range with rocket assistance is 7,500m (8,200yd). Strix, unlike Copperhead, is completely autonomous; once it leaves the muzzle of the mortar the gunners can forget all about it, since it takes charge and finds its own targets.

Bussard

Bussard (or 'buzzard' in English) comes from Germany, having been developed originally by the Diehl company, although in later years the company allied itself with the American firm Lockheed in the hope of interesting the US Army, and changed the name of the device to 'Precision Guided Mortar Munition', or 'PGMM' in order to

Strix, the Swedish anti-tank bomb, in flight.

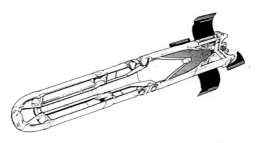

The internal arrangements of Strix, with the seeker head at the front, followed by the guidance electronics and finally the shaped charge at the rear, with a central tube allowing the jet to build up and gather velocity to attack the target.

cater for the American infatuation with acronyms. Bussard was essentially the same sort of thing as Strix, a tubular 120mm body with a powerful shaped charge and an infra-red sensor in the front end. It differs in deploying large wings and steerable fins after reaching the vertex of the trajectory and starting on the downward leg. The original model used the infra-red detector to find a target and compare it with the known charac-teristics of main battle tanks, after which by using the fins and wings it steered and glided to its impact. This was modified after the US Army

displayed an interest and issued specifications of what was desired, and the new and improved PGMM version has two methods of functioning: either in the autonomous mode as described above, or it can be used with the intrepid forward observer and his laser designator, just like Copperhead. The infra-red seeker will detect the laser reflections and home in on them.

Bussard/PGMM weighs just over 17kg (37lbs) and has a maximum range of 15,000m (1,6400yd). No figures for armour penetration have been revealed, but a 120mm shaped charge on the roof of any tank will definitely spoil its day.

Merlin

Merlin was Britain's contribution to the anti-tank mortar challenge and could be thought of as a smaller edition of Bussard so far as shape and action are concerned, thought there was actually no connection whatever between the two designs. It is simply that given the problem, most engineers would be likely to come up with similar solutions; there is not a great deal of room for manoeuvre in the confines of a mortar bomb. And when the mortar in question is of 81mm calibre

Loading Strix into the standard 120mm mortar.

Bussard differs from Strix in having cruciform wings which fold out after leaving the mortar.

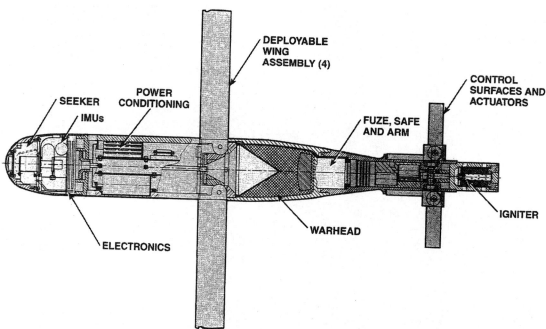

SEEKER

IMUs

POWER CONDITIONING

DEPLOYABLE WING ASSEMBLY (4)

FUZE, SAFE AND ARM

CONTROL SURFACES AND ACTUATORS

IGNITER

WARHEAD

ELECTRONICS

The internals of Bussard; like Strix, it places the shaped charge at the rear end so as to obtain an efficient stand-off distance for the jet.

there is even less room.

British Aerospace began developing Merlin in the mid-1980s in order to give the 81mm L16 mortar an anti-armour capability. Live firing commenced in 1987 and military trials followed.

Eventually the British Army turned it down, principally on the grounds of expense coupled with relatively short range. By that time the US Army had expressed a requirement for a similar weapon, and BAe entered into a partnership with Aliant

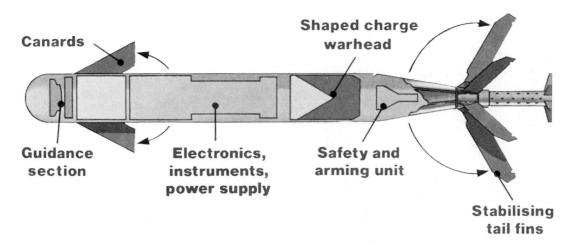

Merlin, the British 81mm anti-armour bomb, used canard wings at the nose and a stabilizing tail of large dimensions, both of which flipped out after leaving the mortar. The layout is similar to other designs, but it used radar for target detection and guidance.

Loading Merlin into the 81mm mortar. The tail unit and cartridge container were discarded after launch, after which the stabilizing tail fins opened.

Techsystems in the USA to offer a 120mm version to the US Army. But the army preferred the Bussard/PGMM design, and with that the Merlin programme was closed down in the late 1990s.

Merlin, like Strix and Bussard, was a long tubular projectile with a shaped charge and a seeker in the nose, but in this case instead of infra-red it used millimetric-wave radar. The bomb was loaded and fired from the 81mm mortar in the normal manner. After launch six rear-mounted fins were deployed to provide stability, and four stub wings were thrust out from

151

the body to give directional control. During the downward flight of the bomb the radar scanned a 300m square area (360sq yd), giving priority to moving targets. Due to the sharp definition of millimetric-wave radar it was almost possible to specify which type of tank to search for, and once a target was recognized the bomb locked on and was then steered to impact by the wings. The maximum range was 420m (460yd), and the penetration, though not as great as that from a 120mm shaped charge, was nevertheless quite satisfactory.

FOMP

And lastly, we come to FOMP, the Fiber-Optic Mortar Projectile. This actually started off as the 107mm GAMP (Guided Anti-armor Mortar Projectile) in the early 1980s, but failed to raise much enthusiasm, so Boeing Defense and Space Group took it away, worked on it, and reintroduced it as the 120mm FOMP, with an 81mm version called IPAW (Infantry Precision Attack Weapon). The projectile is the usual tubular shape with wings that pop out after it has left the mortar, and it also has a rocket motor

which ignites during the upward leg of the trajectory so as to boost the range. But the unique point about FOMP/IPAW is that as it flies through the air it dispenses a fibre-optic cable which is connected to the operator's console alongside the mortar. The front end of the bomb holds a miniature TV camera, and the operator's console has a screen, upon which is a picture of what the bomb sees. The operator can now steer the bomb to the selected target. What the bomb does when it gets there remains to be seen, since at the present time the feasibility of the idea has been demonstrated but the question of what sort of warhead to use has yet to be decided. And in the context of the larger problems of control and so forth, the choice of warhead is a very minor matter.

On the face of it, FOMP/IPAW sounds attractive; my only reservation is that with the bomb approaching the target at something like 450mph the operator is going to have his work cut out to identify and steer to impact with anything smaller than a fairly large aircraft hangar. Trying to pinpoint a foxhole with a persistent enemy machine gun in it would be almost impossible.

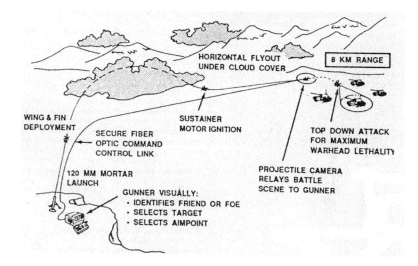

A diagram showing how FOMP will operate, trailing its fibre-optic cable behind it.

Appendix
Comparative Data

Title	Calibre (mm)	Barrel Length (mm)	Elevation (degrees)	Weight in Action (kg)	Bomb Weight (kg)	Muzzle Velocity m/sec	Maximum Range (m)
Argentina							
Current							
MC 1-60 FMK2 Mod 0	60.75	650	45–90	5.80	1.90	127	1,355
MA 1-60 FMK1 Mod 0	60.75	650	45–90	8.0	1.90	170	2,200
MS 1-60 FMK3 Mod 0	60.75	650	40–87	15.57	1.90	205	3,000
LR FMK2 Mod 0	81.4	1,155	40–87	40.6	4.30	290	4,900
LR FMK2 Mod 0	120.18	1,500	45–85	108.5	13.0	336	6,700
Austria							
Obsolete (Austria–Hungary 1914–18)							
Light minenwefer	65	150	45–85	17	4.10		670
Medium granatwerfer	90		45–85	128	23.5		330
Pneumatic minenwerfer m/15	80		5–80		1.25		300
Medium minenwerfer m/15	90	700	30–75	40	5.50		300
Medium minenwerfer m/16	120		45–85		13.0		430
Heavy rifled minenwerfer	140	800	45–66		30.0		620
Pneumatic minenwerfer m/15	150		45.5 fixed	270	6.30		500
Current:							
Commando C6	60.7	640	45–90	5.10	1.65	199	2,600
M8-111	81	1,280	39–84	35.6	4.15	275	6,300
M8-211	81	1,480	39–84	36.60	4.15	296	6,600
M8-522	81	1,280	38–84	42.10	4.15	280	6,400
M12-1111	120.2	1,900	45–85	280	14.5	400	9,000
M12-2222	120.2	1,750	45–85	258	14.5		9,000
M12-3222	120.2	1,900	45–85	260	14.5		9,500
Belgium							
Obsolete							
Lance grenade DBT	51	200	30–50	7.7	0.60	75	585
Current							
PRB NR493	60	780	45–77	22.1	1.36	177	1,800
PRB NR475	81	1,350	40–85	43	4.20	321	5,500
Britain							
Obsolete							
1.57in TH (1915)	4						
2in TH Mk 1 (1915)	51	1,032	45–77	152	27.2	76	455
2in Mk 1 (1935)	51	533	45–90	8.61	0.908		455
3in Stokes (1917)	76	1,290	45–75	49.8	5.7		750
3in Mk 1	76	1,295	45–90	50.8	4.53		2,560
4in Stokes (1918)	107	1,270	45–82	110	11.3	138	933
4.2in Mk 1	107	1,729	45–80	123	9.07		3,750
4.2in Mk 2	107	1,734	45–80	411	9.07		3,750
6in Newton (1917)	152	1,372	40–75	274	20.8		
Livens Projector (1916)	200	838	45 fixed	59	27.2	110	1,257

Title	Calibre (mm)	Barrel Length (mm)	Elevation (degrees)	Weight in Action (kg)	Bomb Weight (kg)	Muzzle Velocity m/sec	Maximum Range (m)
Livens Projector (1917)	200	1,220	45 fixed	81.6	27.2		1,555
9.45in TH (1917)	240	2,450	45–75	3,500	81.0	145	2,150
Current							
51mm L9A1	51.25	543	45–90	6.30	0.92	103	800
81mm L16	81.4	1,280	45–80	36.60	4.47	297	5,800
Bulgaria							
Current							
PIMA M82	82		45–85		3.10		4,100
Chile							
Current							
60mm Commando	60	650	45–90	7.10			1,050
81mm FAMAE	81			3.20			4,200
120mm FAMAE	120			13.0			6,600
China							
Current							
60mm M83-A	60.7	790	45–85	14.7	1.33	204	2,655
60mm Type 63-1	60.75	610	45–85	11.5	1.33	141	1,550
60mm Type WX90	60.75	1,200	45–85	23	1.33	314	5,500
60mm Type WW90-60L	60.75	1,300	45–85	21.5	1.33		6,000
60mm Type WW90-60M	60.75	1,070	45–85	19.86	1.33		5,000
81mm Type W87	81.4		45–85	39.7	4.40		5,700
81mm Type W91	81.4	1,650	45–85	65	4.44		8,000
82mm Type 67	82		45–85	35	3.16	211	3,040
100mm Type 71	100		45–85	74.5	8.0	250	4,750
120mm Type 55	120	1,850	45–80	275	16.6	272	5,700
Czechoslovakia							
Obsolete							
Minomet vz/36	81	1,165	40–80	62	3.2/6.8	220	3,400/1,200
Lehky minomet vz/17	90	810	45–70	132	6.2		1,990
Hruby minomet vz/18	140	1,260	45–75	388	15.0	190	2,680
Current (Czech Republic)							
Konstrukta 81	81		45–95	90	4.56	352	7,000
Egypt							
Current							
Helwan 60	60	610	45–85	12.30	1.75	153	1,530
Helwan M69	82	1,220	45–85	44.5	3.40	205	3,045
Helwan Model UK2	120	1,850	45–85	282	14.0	272	5,520
Finland							
Current							
Vammas 60mm standard	60	720	40–70	16	1.60		2,600
Vammas 60mm long-range	60	940	40–70	18	1.83	258	4,100
Vammas 81mm standard	81	1,305	40–70	40	4.20	300	5,900
Vammas 81mm long-range	81	1,561	40–70	61	4.20	321	6,700
Vammas 120mm light	120.35	1,729	45–80	146	12.8	444	7,300
Vammas 120mm long-range	120.25	2,154	45–80	291	14.9	450	8,600
Vammas 160mm	160.4	3,066	43–70	1,450	40		10,000
France							
Obsolete							
Mortier de 58 T No. 1	58	Spigot	45–80	181	16	67	450
Mortier de 58 T No. 2	58	Spigot	45–80	415	19	102	1,450
Mortier Van Deuren	58	Spigot	45 fixed	350	19.5	78	600

Title	Calibre (mm)	Barrel Length (mm)	Elevation (degrees)	Weight in Action (kg)	Bomb Weight (kg)	Muzzle Velocity m/sec	Maximum Range (m)
Mortier de 75 T	75	?	0–70	215	5.31	130	1,700
Mortier de 150 T, mle 1916	150	1,750	45–75	600	18	145	1,900
Mortier de 150 TM, 1917	150	?	45–72	600	18	160	2,000
Mortier de 240 LT	240	2,450	45–75	3,500	81	145	2,150
Mortier de 240 CT	240	1,532	54–75		81		1,025
Mortier de 310 T	310	?	45–80	3,195	95	150	2,300
5cm Lance granat mle 37	50		45 fixed	3.30	0.450		500
5cm Brandt 60mm mle 35	60.7	724	45–85	17.8	1.30/2.20	158	1,700/950
8cm Brandt 81mm mle 27/31	81.4	1,267	45–85	59.7	3.25/6.50	174	2,850/1,200
8cm Mle 44	81.4	1,158	45–85	64.8	3.50	157	3,010
120mm Cemsa Mle 38	120		45–85	610	16.32		7,300
12cm Mle 51	120	1,738	45–85	320	13.5		6,700
Current							
Brandt 60mm Commando	60	680	45–90	8.90	1.74		1,050
Brandt 60mm proximity	60	860	45–90	6.00	1.74		950
Brandt 60mm light	60	724	40–85	14.80	1.74		2,060
Brandt 60mm long-range	60	1,410	40–85	33.60	2.20		5,000
60mm gun-mortar MCB	60	905	−11– +75		1.74		2,600
60mm gun-mortar LR	60	1,500	−11– +76	75.0	2.2		5,000
Brandt 81mm light	81	1,450	45–85	41.50	4.45		5,600
Brandt 81mm long-range	81	1,895	30–85	93.70	7.10		7,600
81mm gun-mortar MCB	81	2,300	−10– +70	400	7.10		8,000
Brandt MO-120-L light	120	1,632	40–85	84.0	13.0		4,750
Brandt MO-120-M light	120	1,640	40–85	104	19.8		9,000*
Brandt MO-120-LT	120	1,702	45–85	168	14.26	240	7,000
Brandt MO-120-RT rifled	120	2,060	30–85	582	18.60		13,000*
Fly-K TN 8111 (spigot)	51	−	0–85	4.80	0.765		675
* with rocket assistance							

Germany
Obsolete

Title	Calibre (mm)	Barrel Length (mm)	Elevation (degrees)	Weight in Action (kg)	Bomb Weight (kg)	Muzzle Velocity m/sec	Maximum Range (m)
Medium minenwerfer	170			400	50		900
Medium minenwerfer c/1916	170			570	50		1,150
Heavy minenwerfer	240			1,270	98		1,300
Heavy minenwerfer 'Albrecht'	240			1,600	98		2,000
Heavy minenwerfer c/1916	250			750	94		900
5cm GrW 36	50	465	42–90	14.0	0.90	75	520
8cm GrW 34	81.4	1,143	45–90	62.0	3.5	174	2,400
Kurz 8cm GrW 42	81.4	650	40–90	25.2	3.5		1,100
10cm NbW 35	105	1,344	45–90	105	7.38	193	3,025
10cm NbW 40	105	1,858	45–84	800	8.65	310	6,350
10.5cm NbW 51	105	1,260	45–85	651	9.0	271	6,000
12cm GrW 42	120	1,865	45–84	285	15.6	283	6,050
21cm GrW 69 Skoda	210.9	3,000	45–75	2,800	85/110	285/247	5,300/5,190
38cm s LdW(spigot)	168	1,680	37–85	1,600	149	107	1,000

Greece
Current

Title	Calibre (mm)	Barrel Length (mm)	Elevation (degrees)	Weight in Action (kg)	Bomb Weight (kg)	Muzzle Velocity m/sec	Maximum Range (m)
81mm Type E44	81	1,340	45–85	40.90	4.24	261	5,900
120mm Type E56	120		40–85	260			9,000

India
Current

Title	Calibre (mm)	Barrel Length (mm)	Elevation (degrees)	Weight in Action (kg)	Bomb Weight (kg)	Muzzle Velocity m/sec	Maximum Range (m)
51mm E1	51	540	45–90	6.56	0.95	107	850
81mm E1	81	1,550	40–85	135	4.22	217	4,975
120mm E1	120	1,750	45–85	421	12.97	301	6,650

Title	Calibre (mm)	Barrel Length (mm)	Elevation (degrees)	Weight in Action (kg)	Bomb Weight (kg)	Muzzle Velocity m/sec	Maximum Range (m)
Iran							
Current							
60mm Commando T1	60	670	45–85	6.0	1.34	130	1,060
60mm Hadid	60	740	43–85	17.5	1.34	158	2,500
81mm Hadid	81	1,580	43–85	50.5	4.05	270	5,200
120mm Hadid	120	1,730	43–85	138.5	12.97	301	6,200
Iraq							
Current							
60mm Al-Jaleel	60		45–85	22			2,500
82mm Al-Jaleel	82		45–85	63			4,800
120mm Al-Jaleel	120		45–85	148			5,400
Israel							
Current							
52mm IMI	52	490	20–85	7.90	0.94	78	450
60mm Soltam Commando	60	725	45–90	6.70	1.90		1,000
60mm Soltam Standard	60	740	45–85	16.30	1.90	285	2,550
60mm Soltam long-range	60	940	45–85	18.0	1.90	350	4,000
81mm Soltam standard	81	1,560	43–85	42.0	3.90	285	4,900
81mm Soltam long-range	81	1,583	43–85	49.0	4.60	350	6,500
120mm Soltam standard K5	120	1,758	43–85	140	12.60	310	6,200
120mm Soltam long-range K6	120	1,790	43–85	144	13.20	329	7,200
120mm Soltam long-range A7	120	2,154	43–85	387	14.85		9,500
120mm Soltam M65 standard	120	1,950	43–85	231	12.60	325	6,500
160mm Soltam standard	160	3,600	43–70	1,700	40		9,600
Italy							
Obsolete							
Brixia Modello 35	45	260	10–90	15.5	0.465	82	535
Cemsa Modello 939	50		15–45	16.5	0.86		650
Cemsa Modello 40	50		45–65	12.3	0.747	102	820
Cemsa 63mm	63.5		45 fixed	60	2.0		1,400
Cemsa 120mm	120		45–85	830	17.0		72
81/14 Modello 35	81	1,150	40–90	58/4	3.26/6.60	265/135	4,050/1,500
24CM Bombarda	240	2,880	45–80		65.5		
Current							
Breda 81mm	81	1,455	35–85	43.0	4.50		5,000
Japan							
Obsolete							
5cm Type 10	50	241	45–90	2.38	0.54		160
5cm Type 99	50	264	45–90	4.65	0.79		650
5cm Type 98	50	650	40 fixed	22.5	6.40		415
7cm Type 11	70	750	37–77	60.7	2.10		1,555
8cm Type 3	81.4	1,257	45–85	74.8	3.2/6.5		3,300
8cm Type 97	81	1,257	45–85	65.9	3.3/6.5	200	3,000/1,200
8cm Type 99	81	631	45–70	23.7	3.3/6.5		3,000/1,200
9cm Type 94	90	1,270	45–70	155	5.22	227	3,795
9cm Type 97	90	1,330	45–70	105	5.22		3,795
15cm Type 93	150		45–80	253	20.0		2,100
15cm Type 97	150	1,915	45–90	349.6	25.9		2,000

(Currently uses US 60mm and 81mm)

Korea, South							
Current							
60mm KM 181	60	1,000	45–85	19.5	1.47	150	1,795

Title	Calibre (mm)	Barrel Length (mm)	Elevation (degrees)	Weight in Action (kg)	Bomb Weight (kg)	Muzzle Velocity m/sec	Maximum Range (m)
Pakistan							
Current							
60mm Light	60	623	45–80	14.8	1.33	170	2,075
81mm Light	81	1,450	45–85	41.5	3.20	291	4,550
120mm heavy	120	1,740	45–90	402	13.0	331	6,745
Poland							
Obsolete							
Granatnik wz/36	46	396	45–75	12.6	0.76	95	800
Modziercz vz/31	81	1,267	45–85	59.70	3.25/6.5	175	2,850/1,200
Portugal							
Current							
60mm M/9656	650	650	45–85	15.5	1.36	177	2,100
60mm M/968 Commando	60	650	45–90	6.50	1.36	120	1,050
81mm FBP	81	1,455	40–87	46.0	3.25	268	3,837
Romania							
Current							
60mm Commando	60		45–85	7.60	1.60		1,500
60mm standard	60		45–85	23.0	1.60		3,000
82mm standard	82		45–85	43.0	3.10	295	4,500
120mm standard	120		45–80	181	16.39	272	5,775
Russia							
Obsolete							
37mm spade mortar	37	520	Free	2.40	0.68		300
40mm light mortar	40.7		45–80	8.20	0.36	54	700
50mm PM-38	50	780	30 or 60	12.1	0.85	96	800
50mm PM-39	50	775	46–85	15.9	0.85	96	800
50mm PM-40	50	630	45 and 75	9.30	0.85	96	800
50mm PM-41	50	610	45 and 75	10.0	0.85	96	800
82mm PM-36	82	1,320	45–85	62.0	3.40	202	3,000
82mm PM-37	82	1,320	45–85	57.3	3/4	202	3,100
82mm PM-41	82	1,320	45–85	45.0	3.40	202	3,100
82mm PM-43							
107mm PBHM-38	107	1,560	45–80	170.7	8.0	302	6,315
120mm HM-38	120	1,862	45–80	280	16	272	6,000
160mm M-43	160	3,030	45–80	1,170	40.8	245	5,150
Current							
82mm ZB-14	82		45–85	41.9	3.20	220	4,100
82mm 2B9 Vasilek automatic	82		–1–85	632	3.20	270	4,720
120mm M43	120	1,854	45–80	280	16.02	272	5,700
120mm 2S11	120	1,870	45–80	210	16.0	325	7,100
160mm M-160	160	4,550	59–80	1,300	41.5	343	8,040
240mm M-240	240	5,340	45–65	4,150	130.8		9,700
South Africa							
Current							
60mm M4 Commando	60	650	45–90	7.60	1.80	130	1,100
60mm M1	60	650	40–90	17.6	1.80	171	2,100
60mm long-range	60	1,445	40–85	24.0	2.40	325	6,180
81mm M3	81	1,445	45–85	44.40	4.90	363	7,265
Spain							
Obsolete							
5cm Ecia Valero	50		45–80	6.8	0.689		1,000
8cm Mod 933	81		30–85	62.5	4.0/8.57		3,000/1,600
12cm Franco	120		45–70	692	16.5	305	6,400

Title	Calibre (mm)	Barrel Length (mm)	Elevation (degrees)	Weight in Action (kg)	Bomb Weight (kg)	Muzzle Velocity m/sec	Maximum Range (m)
Current							
60mm Model L	60	650	45–85	12.0	2.05		4,600
60mm Model LL	60	1,000	45–85	17.35	2.05		4,600
60mm Commando	60	650	45–90	6.50	2.05		1,200
81mm Model LL	81	1,450	45–85	47.0	4.50	330	6,900
81mm Model LN M86	81	1,150	45–85	41.0	4.50	310	6,200
120mm Model L	120	1,600	45–85	203	14.75	345	8,000
120mm Model M86	120	1,800	45–85	160	14.75	357	8,000
Sweden							
Current							
81mm m.29	81	1,000	45–80	60.0	3.50	190	2,600
120mm m.41C	120	2,000	45–80	285	13.30	317	6,400
Switzerland							
Obsolete							
81mm M1933	81	1,265	45–90	62	3.17	260	4,100
120mm Model 64	81	1,770	45–85	239	14.33	420	8,000
120mm Model 74	120	1,770	45–85	412	14.33	420	8,000
Current							
60mm Model 87	60	845	45–86	7.60	1.85		1,540
81mm Model 72	81	1,280	45–85	45.50	3.17	260	4,100
120mm Model 87	120	1,770	45–85	235	14.38	420	7,500
Turkey							
Current							
60mm MKE Commando	60	650	45–90	8.40	1.36		1,700
81mm MKE UTI	81	1,453	40–85	66.50	4.82	331	5,800
81mm MKE NTI	81	1,150	40–85	59.50	4.82		3,120
120mm MKE HY12	120	1,900	35–85	570	17.0	366	8,180
USA							
Obsolete							
60mm M1	60	726	40–85	19.0	1.33	178	1,840
81mm M1	81	1,257	40–85	61.6	3.12	213	3,010
105mm T13	105	1,880	45–85	86.4	15.9		4,000
4.2in M1	107	1,018	45–60	150	11.1	256	3,985
155mm T25	155	1,830	45–85	259	28.83		2,295
Current							
60mm M2	60	726	40–85	19.07	1.36	158	1,815
60mm M19	60	819	40–85	21.03	1.77	350	2,170
81mm M29	81	1,295	45–85	45.0	4.23		4,595
81mm M252	81	1,277	45–85	42.32	4.31	268	4,800
107mm M30	107	1,524	40–59	305	12.28	292	5,425
120mm M120	120	1,758	40–85	144.7	14.97	450	10,000
Yugoslavia							
Current							
50mm M8	50		45–90	7.30	1.05	80	480
60mm M-70	60	650	45–85	7.60	1.35		1,630
60mm M57	60	725	45–85	19.85	1.35	160	1,700
60mm M90 long-range	60	1,325	42–85	13.26	2.10		5,200
81mm M68	81	1,640	45–85	41.50	3.05	300	5,000
82mm M69A	82	1,200	45–85	45.0	3.06		4,945
81mm M69B	81	1,450	45–85	48.6	4.10	310	6,050
120mm UBM 52	120	1,200	45–85	400	12.25	297	6,000
120mm M74 light	120	1,690	45–85	120	12.25	266	6,215
120mm M75 light	120	1,690	45–85	177	12.25	290	9,400*

* with rocket assistance

Index